MUSIC THEORY
ESSENTIAL GUIDE

JULIA WINTERSON
with PAUL HARRIS

FABER *ff* MUSIC   EDITION PETERS

Acknowledgements

I am grateful to Barry Russell for his help and advice.
My thanks are also due to the music technology and pop
students at the University of Huddersfield.

Julia Winterson

© 2014 by Faber Music Ltd and Peters Edition Limited
First published in 2014 by Faber Music Ltd and Peters Edition Limited

ISBN: 978-0-571-53632-8
FP: 3001

Cover artwork by Dominic Brookman
Music processed by MusicSet 2000
Design by Susan Clarke
Printed in England by Caligraving Ltd

Peters Edition Limited
2–6 Baches Street
London N1 6DN

Faber Music Ltd
Bloomsbury House
74–77 Great Russell Street
London WC1B 3DA

To buy Edition Peters publications or to find out about the full range of titles available
please contact your local music retailer or Edition Peters sales enquiries:
Tel: +44 (0)20 7553 4000   Fax: +44 (0)20 7490 4921
E-mail: sales@editionpeters.com   Website: www.editionpeters.com

To buy Faber Music publications or to find out about the full range of titles available
please contact your local music retailer or Faber Music sales enquiries:
Tel: +44 (0)1279 828982   Fax: +44 (0)1279 828983
E-mail: sales@fabermusic.com   Website: fabermusicstore.com

All rights reserved.

Contents

Rhythm *1*

Pitch *19*

Scales *35*

Harmony *49*

Transposition *65*

Instruments and voices *73*

Working with rhythm, melody and words *91*

Ornaments *101*

Terms and signs *109*

Appendix 1: Table of scales and modes *119*

Appendix 2: Further listening *124*

Appendix 3: Periods in music history *128*

Glossary of common musical terms *130*

Index *138*

Foreword

What springs to mind when you hear the words 'music theory'? Boredom? Hard work? Something to endure in order to get through examinations? If so, you are not alone! Many musicians underplay the relationship between music *in theory* and music *in practice*. But that connection is not only very real but also absolutely vital: without a solid appreciation of what constitutes music, and an understanding of how its 'ingredients' can be manipulated and transformed, can one really be a complete musician?

Music Theory: the essential guide is a practical and relevant introduction to music through the lens of music theory: it explores the key musical ingredients, concepts and facts essential for anyone wishing to flourish as a musician. By constantly making connections to real music through notated examples, listening suggestions and guidance on composition and transposition, this book is in fact about music in its entirety, not just music *in theory*.

Equally, however, it fully supports the requirements of the ABRSM music theory examinations (Grades 1 to 5), as well as anyone taking GCSE, B-TECH, AS and A Level music examinations. Whether you're a student, teacher or simply a musician with a desire to deepen your musical understanding, I hope you find this book as fascinating and indispensable as I do.

Paul Harris, September 2014

About the authors

Julia Winterson studied performance at the Royal Academy of Music and completed a DPhil in Music at the University of York. She now combines music lecturing at the University of Huddersfield with freelance writing and research. She has worked as the Head of New Music for Peters Edition and as Music Qualification Leader for a national examination board – this involved the development of music qualifications including A Level, GCSE, BTEC and HND. Publications include seven anthologies of music for schools, *Pop Music: The Text Book* and numerous articles for music magazines and academic journals.

Paul Harris is one of the most sought-after music educationalists, renowned for his innovative Simultaneous Learning approach. He has over 600 publications to his name, including *The Virtuoso Teacher*, *The Practice Process*, *Simultaneous Learning* and the highly acclaimed *Improve your ...* series. Paul writes frequently on music education and is in great demand as a workshop and seminar leader around the world.

Rhythm

'Rhythm is everywhere. Rhythm has existed since before man evolved: it is an elemental force. There's the rhythm of life: our heartbeat, our pulse, breathing, walking along at a steady pace. The rhythm of nature: night and day, time itself. The rhythm of words: speech and poetry. The rhythm of the modern world: machinery, transport, a clock ticking. Rhythm is all about repetitive patterns of sound or movement; it is, in fact, the heartbeat of music. It includes pulse, relative length of notes, a sense of emphasis, and the general sense of motion that causes music (and life) to move forward.'

Paul Harris

2 Rhythm

Notes and rests

The word 'rhythm' describes the way that sounds are grouped together in different patterns over time. These patterns are produced by **notes** (sounds) and **rests** (silences) of different lengths. Musical notation is used to represent sounds as notes written on a staff or stave (see page 20). While the *position* of a note on the stave shows its **pitch** (see page 19), the *shape* of the note shows its **duration** – the length of time it lasts in relation to other notes. **Rests** are used to represent silence.

longer duration ↑

British name	American name	Note	Rest
Semibreve	Whole note	𝅝	𝄻
Minim	Half note	𝅗𝅥 or 𝅗𝅥	𝄼
Crotchet	Quarter note	𝅘𝅥 or 𝅘𝅥	𝄽
Quaver	Eighth note	𝅘𝅥𝅮 or 𝅘𝅥𝅮	𝄾
Semiquaver	Sixteenth note	𝅘𝅥𝅯 or 𝅘𝅥𝅯	𝄿
Demisemiquaver	Thirty-second note	𝅘𝅥𝅰 or 𝅘𝅥𝅰	𝅀

↓ *shorter duration*

Two notes that are found less frequently are the **breve** or **double whole note** 𝅜 (or ||𝅗𝅥||) and the **hemidemisemiquaver** or **sixty-fourth note** 𝅘𝅥𝅱.

> Semibreve and minim rests look similar: the minim rest sits above the line and the semibreve rest hangs below the line. It might help to think that the minim rest is floating (because it is smaller) and the semibreve rest has sunk (because it is bigger).

British name		American name
1 semibreve	𝆩	1 whole note
= 2 minims	𝅗𝅥	= 2 half notes
= 4 crotchets	♩	= 4 quarter notes
= 8 quavers	♪	= 8 eighth notes
= 16 semiquavers		= 16 sixteenth notes
= 32 demisemiquavers		= 32 thirty-second notes

The relative durations of note-values

Dotted notes

The duration of notes and rests can be lengthened by adding dots.
A single dot placed after a note or rest adds half again to its original value:

Notes

♪. = ♪ + ♫

♪. = ♪ + ♫

♩. = ♩ + ♪

𝅗𝅥. = 𝅗𝅥 + ♩

o. = o + 𝅗𝅥

Rests

𝄾. = 𝄾 + 𝄿

𝄾. = 𝄾 + 𝄿

𝄽. = 𝄽 + 𝄾

𝄼. = 𝄼 + 𝄽

𝄻. = 𝄻 + 𝄼

A second dot adds a further quarter to the note or rest's original value.
When two dots are used, it is said to be **double-dotted**.

Notes

♪.. = ♪ + ♫ + ♬

♪.. = ♪ + ♫ + ♬

♩.. = ♩ + ♪ + ♫

𝅗𝅥.. = 𝅗𝅥 + ♩ + ♪

o.. = o + 𝅗𝅥 + ♩

Rests

𝄾.. = 𝄾 + 𝄿 + 𝄿

𝄾.. = 𝄾 + 𝄿 + 𝄿

𝄽.. = 𝄽 + 𝄾 + 𝄿

𝄼.. = 𝄼 + 𝄽 + 𝄾

𝄻.. = 𝄻 + 𝄼 + 𝄽

Tied notes

The duration of a note can also be increased by tying one note-value to another of the same pitch. A tie ⌣ is a curved line that adds the values of both notes together to make one sustained note. A tie is often used to join notes that are sustained across a **bar-line** or **measure** (see 'Bars and bar-lines' below).

𝅗𝅥 ⌣ 𝅗𝅥 = 𝅗𝅥 + 𝅗𝅥 = 𝅗𝅥.

♩ ⌣ ♪ = ♩ + ♪ = ♩.

> There are rules governing when to use ties and when to use dotted notes (see page 13). Ties are never used on rests.

Bars and bar-lines

Music is divided up into **bars** (sometimes known as **measures**) that contain a specified number of **beats**. The bars are separated by **bar-lines**.

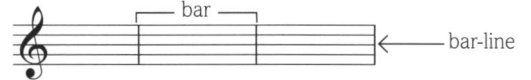

The word **pulse** is used to describe the underlying beat in a piece of music. When we beat time to a piece of music we are marking the main beats in a bar – the strongest accent is on the first beat. Music with:
- **two** beats in a bar is in **duple time**.
- **three** beats in a bar is in **triple time**.
- **four** beats in a bar is in **quadruple time**.

A beat may have the duration of a minim, crotchet, quaver, or any other note-value. The most common beat-value is the crotchet.

Introducing time signatures

The time signature is found at the beginning of a piece of music immediately *after* the key signature (see page 38). It tells you:
- the **number** of beats in each bar
- the **note-value** of the beat.

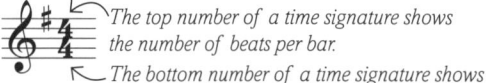

The top number of a time signature shows the number of beats per bar.

The bottom number of a time signature shows the note-value of the beat: 2 = ♩ *beat*   4 = ♩ *beat*   8 = ♪ *beat*

Unlike the key signature, the time signature is not found at the beginning of every line of music. If the time signature stays the same throughout a piece, it is only written once. However, if the time of the music changes, a new time signature is needed.

> Time signatures have been used in Western music since about 1700.

Simple time signatures

Simple time signatures usually use a quaver, a crotchet, a minim, or another un-dotted note as the main beat. This means that the beats are divisible into halves, e.g.:

Depending on the number of main beats in a bar, simple time can be further grouped into **simple duple** (two beats), **simple triple** (three beats) and **simple quadruple** (four beats):

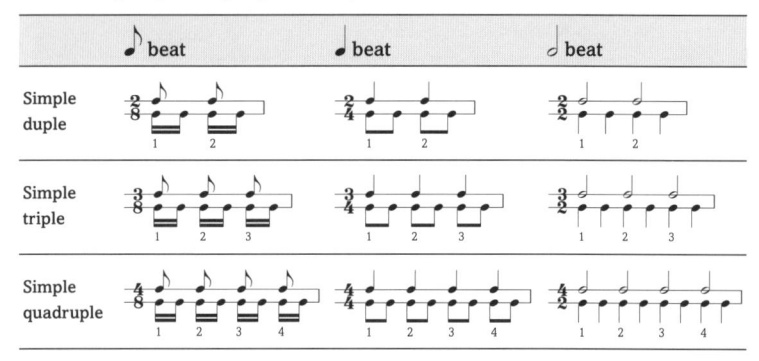

	♪ beat	♩ beat	♩ beat
Simple duple	2/8	2/4	2/2
Simple triple	3/8	3/4	3/2
Simple quadruple	4/8	4/4	4/2

Notice the difference between the time signatures $\frac{2}{4}$ and the relatively rare $\frac{4}{8}$. Although they both use four quavers in a bar, $\frac{2}{4}$ has two crotchet beats per bar and $\frac{4}{8}$ has four quaver beats per bar.

Common time and split common time

$\frac{4}{4}$ (four crotchets beats in a bar) is the most common time signature and is also known as **common time**. This is sometimes shown by a letter **C**:

The sign ¢ indicates $\frac{2}{2}$ (two minim beats in a bar). It is often referred to as **split common time**.

Compound time signatures

Compound time signatures use a dotted note as the main beat; this is often a dotted crotchet. $\frac{6}{8}$, $\frac{9}{8}$ and $\frac{12}{8}$ are all compound time signatures with dotted crotchet beats. In compound time signatures, the dotted beat is divisible by three:

- When the main beat is a dotted crotchet, the quavers are grouped in threes (as above).
- When the main beat is a dotted minim, the crotchets are grouped in threes.
- When the main beat is a dotted quaver, the semiquavers are grouped in threes.

Depending on the number of main beats in a bar, compound time can be further categorised into **compound duple** (two dotted beats), **compound triple** (three dotted beats) and **compound quadruple** (four dotted beats):

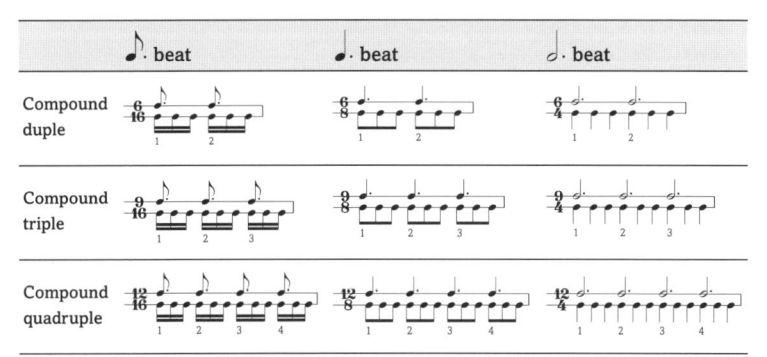

Notice the difference between the time signatures $\frac{3}{4}$ and $\frac{6}{8}$. Although they both use six quavers in a bar, $\frac{3}{4}$ has three crotchet beats per bar and $\frac{6}{8}$ has two dotted crotchet beats per bar. Here is the same passage using the same note-values, but written in $\frac{3}{4}$ and $\frac{6}{8}$:

Stravinsky's 1913 ballet *The Rite of Spring* is renowned for its rhythmic energy. In the final number, 'The Sacrificial Dance' the time signature changes five times in the opening seven bars: $\frac{3}{16} - \frac{2}{16} - \frac{3}{16} - \frac{2}{8} - \frac{2}{16} - \frac{3}{16}$

Time signatures with irregular divisions

All of the above time signatures have regular divisions into two, three or four beats per bar. Occasionally time signatures are used that have irregular divisions.

> Irregular metres are often found in folk music.

Quintuple time

In $\frac{5}{4}$ and $\frac{5}{8}$ the five beats are grouped into either 2 + 3 or 3 + 2. A well-known piece in $\frac{5}{4}$ is the second movement of Tchaikovsky's Symphony No. 6 – *Pathétique*. In this passage the beats are divided into 2 + 3:

Extract from Allegro con grazia *(II) from Symphony No. 6 (1893) by Tchaikovsky*

> In his opera *Orlando* (1733), Handel included several bars in $\frac{5}{8}$ in the middle of a $\frac{4}{4}$ passage to represent his hero's madness when suffering from unrequited love.

Septuple time

In $\frac{7}{4}$ and $\frac{7}{8}$ the seven beats can be grouped into various combinations of two, three and four, e.g. 2 + 3 + 2, or 3 + 2 + 2, or 4 + 3. Pieces in septuple time were quite rare before the twentieth century; however, French composer Alkan wrote a piano piece in $\frac{7}{4}$, *Air à 7 temps*, in 1849:

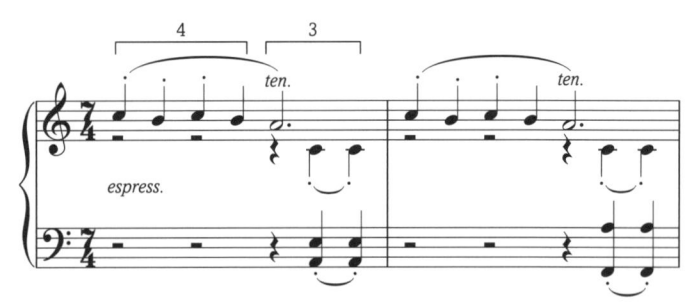

Extract from 'Air à 7 temps' from Deuxième recueil, *Op. 32 No. 8 (1849) by Alkan*

'The Alcotts', the third movement of Charles Ives' *Concord Sonata* (1912) includes a bar with the time signature of $\frac{4\frac{1}{2}}{4}$ – four and a half crotchet beats.

Béla Bartók's *Six Dances in Bulgarian Rhythm* (1926–39) are based on folk music and use asymmetrical dance rhythms. The time signatures are written as the sum of smaller groups. For instance, No. 1 has a time signature of $\frac{4+3+3}{8}$.

Grouping notes and rests

Notes and rests are grouped together in ways that make it easier to see where the beats are, so that the music is clearer to read. For example:

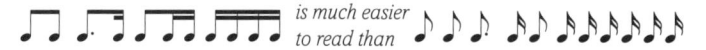

♩♩ ♩.♩ ♩♩♩ ♩♩♩♩ *is much easier to read than* ♪ ♪ ♪ ♪♪ ♪♪♪♪♪

There are certain standard conventions that are usually followed when grouping notes and rests.

Grouping notes in simple time

Beams

In $\frac{2}{4}$, $\frac{3}{4}$ and $\frac{4}{4}$, notes belonging to the same crotchet beat should be beamed together so that the beats can be clearly picked out by the eye.

♫ or ♬

A crotchet beat made up of demisemiquavers can be grouped in either of two ways:

The beamed notes do not have to be of the same duration:

A beam should not normally extend beyond a beat as it becomes difficult to see where the beat divisions are:

Correct   Incorrect

However, it is acceptable to beam together complete bars of quavers in $\frac{2}{4}$ or $\frac{3}{4}$:

Complete bars of semiquavers in $\frac{3}{8}$ may also be beamed together:

In $\frac{4}{4}$, complete bars of quavers should be beamed into two groups of four. They should not be grouped together as this would make the music more difficult to read.

Correct   Incorrect

The same applies to bars in $\frac{4}{4}$ containing mixed note-values: beams should be avoided across the middle of the bar so that the two halves of the bar are clearly indicated:

Correct   Incorrect

Correct   Incorrect

> When grouping notes in $\frac{4}{4}$, it may help to think of an invisible line down the middle of the bar.

Ties

In simple time, ties between notes should be avoided where possible:

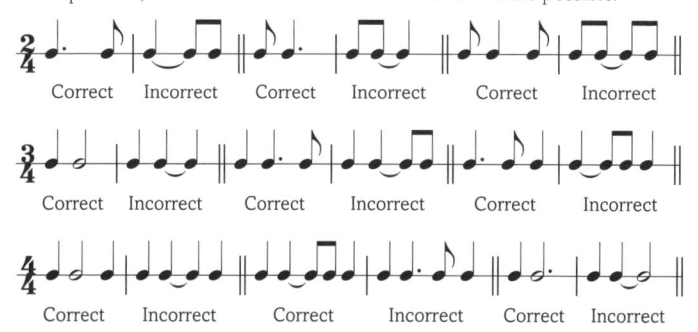

Correct   Incorrect   Correct   Incorrect   Correct   Incorrect

Correct   Incorrect   Correct   Incorrect   Correct   Incorrect

Correct   Incorrect   Correct   Incorrect   Correct   Incorrect

Music examples

The following musical examples illustrate some of the ways in which notes are grouped together in simple time.

Extract from Klavier Sonata in A minor K149 (c.1752) by Domenico Scarlatti

Extract from 'Minuet' from French Suite No. III in B minor (1722) by J. S. Bach

Extract from 'Allegro' from Suite No. 3 in D minor (1733) by Handel

Extract from Piano Sonata Op. 53 ('Waldstein') (1804) by Beethoven

Grouping notes in compound time

Beams

In $\frac{6}{8}$, $\frac{9}{8}$ and $\frac{12}{8}$, notes shorter than a dotted crotchet should be beamed together so that the beats can be clearly picked out by the eye. Notes belonging to the same dotted crotchet beat are beamed together:

Extract from Fugue *by John Blow (1649–1708)*

Here are some common groupings of quavers, dotted quavers and semiquavers in compound time. All of them are grouped into dotted crotchet beats:

Quavers and shorter notes are beamed in such a way that the dotted-beat groupings are clear:

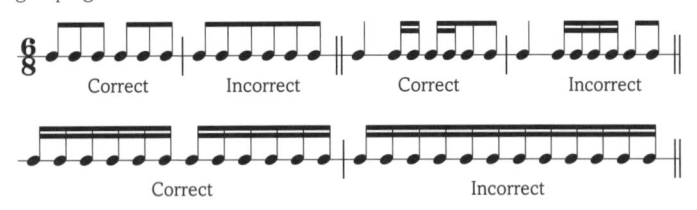

Ties

In compound time, ties are often necessary in order to notate the rhythmic duration of a note. The following passage would be impossible to write without using ties:

Ties between notes in compound time are also used to signpost where the main (dotted) beats are:

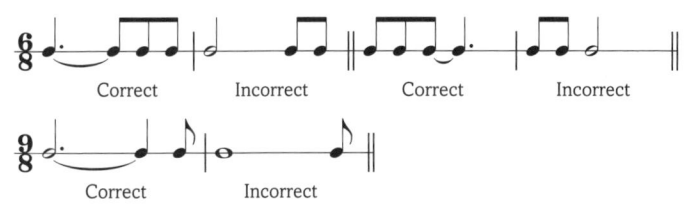

Notes lasting a whole bar are written as follows in $^6_8$, $^9_8$ and $^{12}_8$:

Notice that a tie is required to notate a whole-bar note in $^9_8$.

> Composers do not always follow these rules, so you may be able to find unconventional groupings in the pieces you are playing.

Grouping rests in simple time

In general, every main beat should have a rest of its own – rests of longer than a beat should be avoided. Thus:

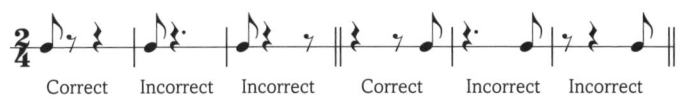

However, a clear half-bar at the beginning or end of a bar in $^4_4$ can be shown by a minim rest:

Grouping rests in compound time

In compound time, one rest may be used for the first and second divisions of the beat together, but not for the second and third together:

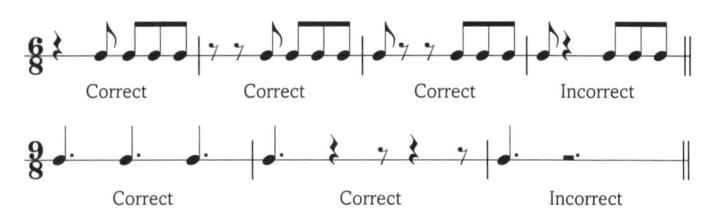

In $\frac{6}{8}$, $\frac{9}{8}$ and $\frac{12}{8}$, a silence lasting for a dotted crotchet beat may have a rest of its own 𝄼· or be shown as 𝄼 𝄾 , although the former is generally considered clearer. Rests that are longer than a beat should be avoided:

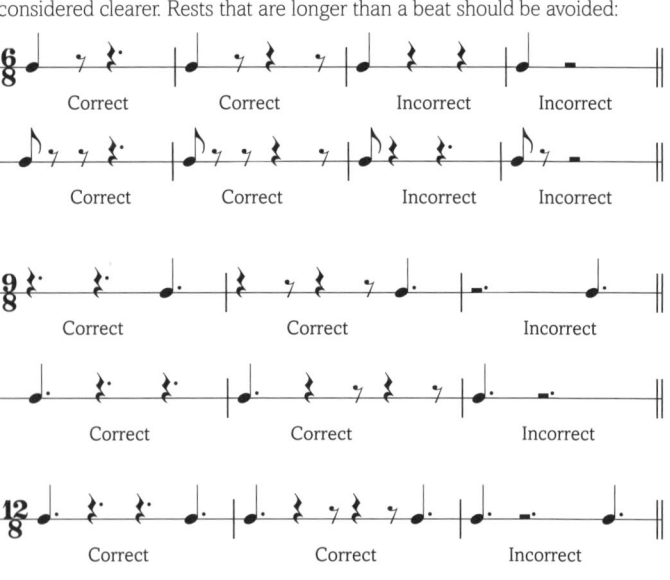

A clear half-bar at the beginning or end of a bar in $\frac{12}{8}$ can be shown by a dotted minim rest:

Whole-bar rests

A whole-bar rest is always shown by a semibreve rest, whatever the time signature:

Irregular note groupings

Irregular note groupings are sometimes found within a regular pulse. Commonly used irregular groupings are **duplets**, **triplets**, **quintuplets** and **sextuplets**.

Triplets and duplets

Beats are divisible into halves in simple time and into thirds in compound time. However, sometimes a composer may wish to divide a beat up into thirds in simple time – i.e. so that three notes are played in the time of two. Such subdivisions are called triplets. The triplet is indicated by the number *3* above or below the notes to which they apply. Triplet quavers and semiquavers are beamed together; triplet crotchets and minims are grouped with a bracket ⌐¬ or, less commonly today, a slur ⌒ above or below the notes.

Extract from Impromptu No. 2 in E flat, *D.899 (1829) by Schubert*

Triplets are not always made up of notes of the same value. In the following example, bar 3 uses triplets made up of a crotchet and a quaver:

Extract from The Liberty Bell *(1893) by Sousa*

Sometimes a composer may wish to divide a beat up into halves in compound time – i.e. so that two notes are played in the time of three. Such subdivisions are called **duplets**. The duplet is indicated by the number 2 above or below the notes. Duplet quavers and semiquavers are beamed together; duplet crotchets and minims are grouped with a bracket ⌐¬ or, less commonly today, a slur ⌒ above or below the notes.

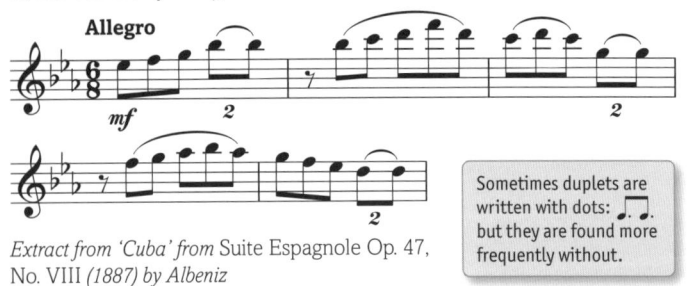

Extract from 'Cuba' from Suite Espagnole Op. 47, No. VIII *(1887) by Albeniz*

> Sometimes duplets are written with dots: ♩.♩. but they are found more frequently without.

Other irregular note groupings

The other irregular note groups found most frequently are **quintuplets** (5), **sextuplets** (6) and **septuplets** (7). In every case, the irregular note group is played in the time of a simple-time note-value – i.e. a quaver, a crotchet or a minim.

Extract from 'Allegro appassionato' from Clarinet Sonata Op. 120, No. 1 *(1894) by Brahms*

In this extract, quintuplets, sextuplets and septuplets are written in semiquavers, as each of the groupings takes place over the time of a crotchet (or four-semiquaver) beat.

Quadruplets, where four notes are played in time of three, are usually found in compound time. They are shown by the figure '4' placed above or below the four notes:

> **Irregular note-groupings: some guidelines**
>
> Irregular note-groups are written in values where the ratio is a contracting one. Thus:
>
> - Triplets are written in values applicable to two of the same kind – 3:2.
> - Quintuplets, sextuplets and septuplets are written in values applicable to four of the same kind – 5:4, 6:4, 7:4.
> - 9, 10, 11, 13 and 15-note groups are written in values applicable to eight of the same kind – 9:8, 10:8, etc.

Syncopation

Syncopation is the effect created when off-beat notes are accented. It can be produced in the following ways:

- **By placing a stress on a weak beat or between beats.** In the following example, Dvořák puts the emphasis between the first and second beat in bars 1 and 5.

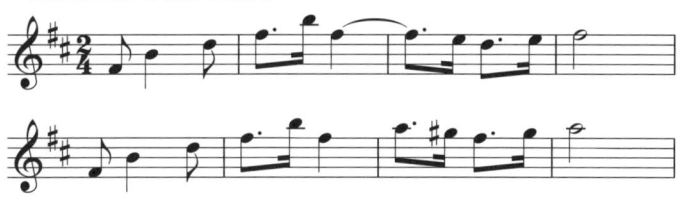

Extract from Slavonic Dance *Op. 72 No. 1 (1886) by Dvořák*

- **By beginning a note on a weak beat and holding it over onto a strong beat.** Scott Joplin begins a note on the final (weak) quaver beat of bar 1 and ties it over onto the first (strong) beat of bar 2:

Extract from The Entertainer *(1902) by Scott Joplin*

- **By putting a rest on a normally strong beat.** Mozart opens the final movement of the 'Prague' symphony with a rest. This has the effect of displacing the beat of the music that follows.

Extract from Symphony No. 38 (the 'Prague', III) *(1787) by Mozart*

> ### Hemiolas
>
> A hemiola is a device frequently found in music up to and including the Baroque period. It occurs when three beats are performed in the time of two, or two beats are performed in the time of three, and creates a syncopated effect. In the following example, the music is principally in triple time (with three minim beats), but switches to duple time (two dotted minim beats) in bars 2 and 8 to produce a hemiola.
>
> Though A - ma - ryl - lis dance in green   like fai - ry   queen
>
> And sing full__ clear   Co - rin - na   can with smil - ing cheer
>
> *Extract from 'Though Amaryllis dance in green' (Madrigal for five voices) (1588) by William Byrd*

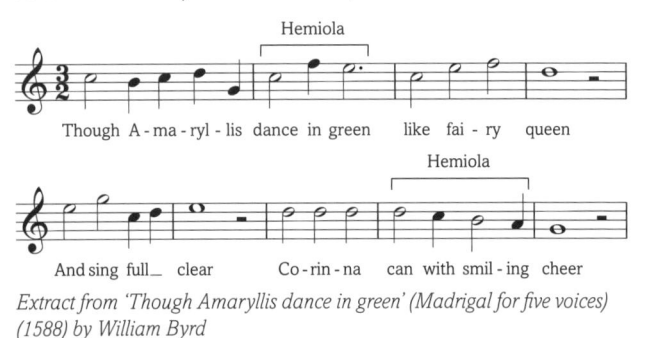

Pitch

'What makes a tune tuneful? We have rhythm, but we need another ingredient. The answer is, of course, pitch. Pitch is the word we use to describe high and low sounds and it is the ingredient that turns rhythm into melody. Pitch is anything to do with the range of notes that combine to make those tunes sound tuneful. What makes a 'good' tune is an interesting question! Something to ponder on …'

Paul Harris

The stave

In music, the word **pitch** is used to describe how high or low a sound is. Each pitch is classified as a particular note that can be represented visually through music notation. Sounds of different pitches are represented as **notes** that are placed on a **stave** (or **staff**). The five-lined stave consists of five parallel lines with four equal spaces between them.

The five-lined stave

Higher pitch
⇕
Lower pitch

Notes are positioned on the lines or in the spaces: the higher up a note is positioned on the stave, the higher the pitch; the lower down, the lower the pitch.

Note names

Notes are named, in ascending order, by the first seven letters of the alphabet: A up to G. These letter names are then repeated to represent equivalent notes at a higher or lower level (or 'octave' – see page 26).

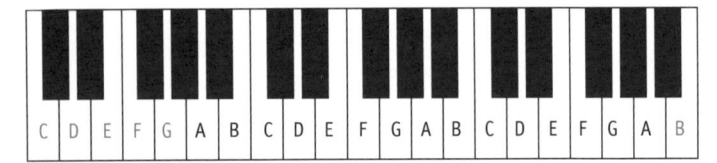

Lower pitch   *Higher pitch*

Piano keyboard showing note names

Treble clef

Clefs are written at the start of the stave and tell you what pitches (or notes), are being shown. When the **treble clef** sign (𝄞) is used, the note names are as follows:

> The treble clef is sometimes known as the G clef because the clef curls around the note G.

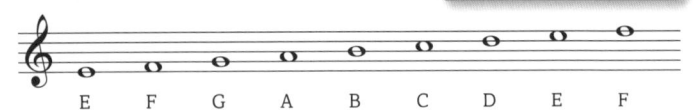

E F G A B C D E F

When the treble clef is used:

- the notes on the lines are E, G, B, D, F.
- the notes in the spaces are F, A, C, E.

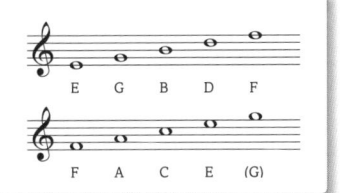

Bass clef

A different clef is used to write lower notes: 𝄢. This is known as the **bass clef**. When the bass clef is used, the note names are as follows:

> The bass clef is sometimes known as the F clef because the two dots are on either side of the note F.

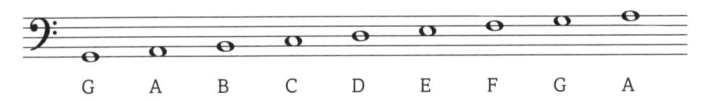

G A B C D E F G A

When the bass clef is used:

- the notes on the lines are G, B, D, F, A.
- the notes in the spaces are A, C, E, G.

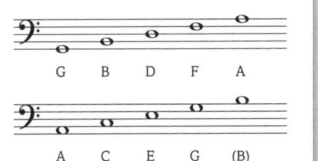

Middle C

The C nearest the centre of the piano keyboard is often referred to as **middle C**. It is also the pitch that falls exactly between the bottom of the treble clef and the top of the bass clef:

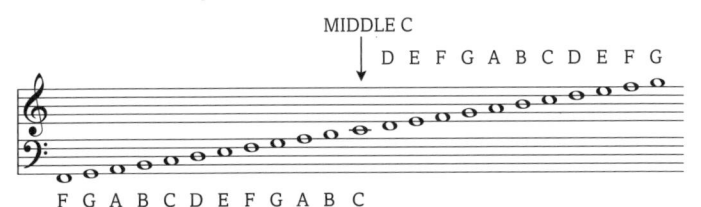

MIDDLE C

D E F G A B C D E F G

F G A B C D E F G A B C

Ledger lines

Ledger lines are short lines above or below the stave; they are used whenever the note is too high or too low to be written on the stave. In the treble and bass clef, middle C is written with a ledger line.

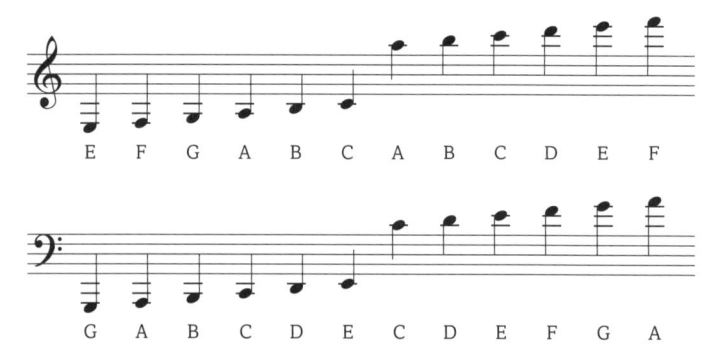

E F G A B C A B C D E F

G A B C D E C D E F G A

Notes with ledger lines in the treble and bass clefs

Stems

Many note symbols have a **stem**; how stems are positioned relates directly to where a note is positioned on the stave. When a note is pitched:

- above the middle line of the stave, the stem points downwards and joins to the left of the note head.

- below the middle line of the stave, the stem points upwards and joins to the right of the note head.

- on the middle line of the stave, the stem may point either upwards or downwards.

Alto and tenor clefs

The most commonly used clefs are the treble (G) clef and the bass (F) clef. Two other clefs that are in regular use today are the **alto clef**: 𝄡 and the **tenor clef**: 𝄡. These are both C clefs because the line they are centred on is middle C.

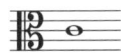

The alto clef is used by the viola.

Middle C written in the alto clef

The tenor clef is used by cellos, double basses, bassoons and tenor trombones when they are playing in their upper register but they use the bass clef most of the time.

Middle C written in the tenor clef

Here is the same melody written at the same pitch in the four different clefs:

Treble clef

Alto clef

Tenor clef

Bass clef

Extract from Beethoven's Ode to Joy *(Symphony No. 9)*

Accidentals: sharps, flats and naturals

Each note written on a stave can have its pitch slightly raised or lowered by the addition of an **accidental**.

A **sharp** (♯) placed before a note raises its pitch by one semitone (see page 36).

A **flat** (♭) lowers its pitch by one semitone.

A **natural** (♮) restores a note, previously sharpened or flattened, to its original pitch.

D sharp (raised)   *D flat (lowered)*   *D natural (restored)*

Notes that sound the same but are written (or 'spelt') differently are said to be **enharmonic**. For instance C♯ and D♭ are enharmonic equivalents.

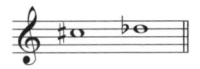

Theory in practice: using accidentals

Here are some guidelines for you to follow when you are reading or writing music:

- Accidentals are written before the note, even though we say them after (e.g. 'B flat').
- Accidentals remain in effect until the end of the bar, unless cancelled or overwritten by a subsequent sign.
- Accidentals *do not* apply to the same note at a different octave or in a different part.
- Accidentals on tied notes remain in effect until the end of the tied note, even where the note is sustained over a bar line.

- To restore a note to its original pitch, the accidental is cancelled by the appropriate natural, flat or sharp sign.
- Double flats and double sharps are cancelled in the same way. Note that only one natural sign is needed.

Double flats and double sharps

Sometimes it is necessary to sharpen a note that has already been sharpened, or to flatten a note that has already been flattened.

- A **double sharp** (𝄪) placed before a note raises its pitch by two semitones.

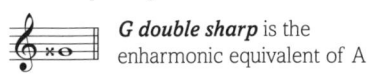

  G double sharp is the enharmonic equivalent of A

- A **double flat** (𝄫) lowers its pitch by two semitones.

  A double flat is the enharmonic equivalent of G

> A double sharp is used in the G sharp minor scale, where the seventh (G♯) is sharpened a further semitone to become G double sharp.

Intervals

An **interval** is the distance between two notes. If two notes are played together they form a **harmonic interval**; if they are played separately, they form a **melodic interval**.

harmonic interval

melodic interval

Intervals are measured by the total number of letter names found, starting with the lower note and going up to the higher note. Thus:

- C up to D is a **2nd**.
- C up to E (C D E) is a **3rd**.

> Both notes of the interval are included in the count.

Intervals in the major scale

All major scales (see page 36) are made from the same pattern of intervals. There are two kinds of intervals in the major scale: major intervals and perfect intervals.

Major intervals: 2nd (a tone), 3rd, 6th and 7th

Perfect intervals: 4th, 5th and octave.
Perfect intervals have a pure, rather hollow sound.

> There is no such thing as a major 4th or major 5th.

Here are the names of all of the intervals found between the tonic (key-note) of C major and the other degrees of the C major scale.

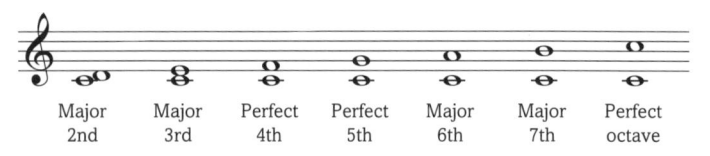

| Major | Major | Perfect | Perfect | Major | Major | Perfect |
| 2nd | 3rd | 4th | 5th | 6th | 7th | octave |

Other intervals

Either of the notes forming an interval may be sharpened or flattened to create a different kind of interval.

Minor intervals

Major intervals become **minor** when they are decreased by a semitone:

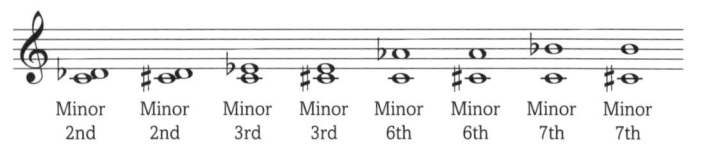

| Minor | Minor | Minor | Minor | Minor | Minor | Minor | Minor |
| 2nd | 2nd | 3rd | 3rd | 6th | 6th | 7th | 7th |

> A minor 2nd is the same interval as a semitone (see page 36).

Diminished intervals

Perfect intervals become **diminished** when they are decreased by a semitone:

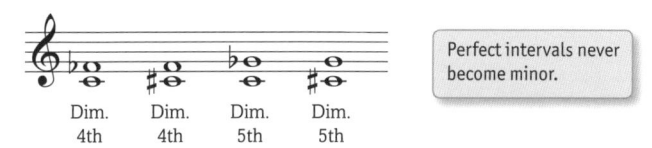

Dim. 4th | Dim. 4th | Dim. 5th | Dim. 5th

> Perfect intervals never become minor.

Minor 3rds and 7ths may be further flattened by a semitone and become **diminished**:

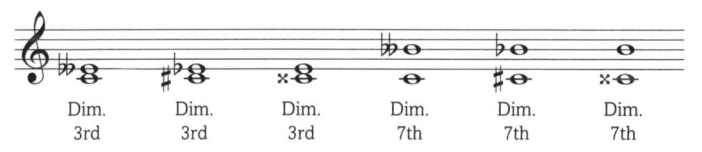

Dim. 3rd | Dim. 3rd | Dim. 3rd | Dim. 7th | Dim. 7th | Dim. 7th

Augmented intervals

Major 2nds and 6ths and all perfect intervals become **augmented** when they are increased by a semitone:

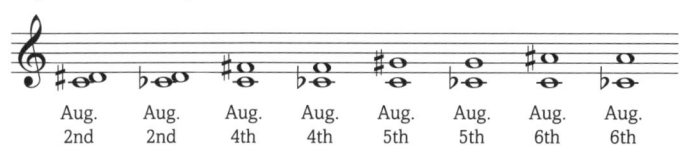

Aug. 2nd | Aug. 2nd | Aug. 4th | Aug. 4th | Aug. 5th | Aug. 5th | Aug. 6th | Aug. 6th

The tritone

The interval of the augmented 4th or diminished 5th is made up of three tones (C to D, D to E, E to F♯/G♭) and is therefore known as a **tritone**:

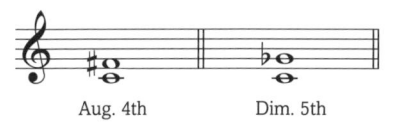

Aug. 4th | Dim. 5th

> The tritone is sometimes known as the *diabolus in musica* or 'the devil's interval' because of its dissonant, unstable quality.

Theory in practice: naming and writing intervals

The intervals found between the tonic (key-note) of a major key and the other degrees of the scale serve as a useful standard by which other intervals can be worked out.

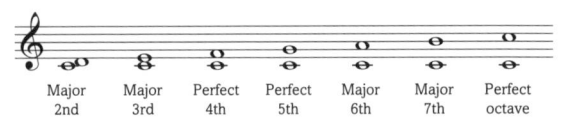

Major	Major	Perfect	Perfect	Major	Major	Perfect
2nd	3rd	4th	5th	6th	7th	octave

Always name the interval from the lower note. Think of the lower note as though it is the tonic or key-note.

Example 1: G to D

To name this interval, think of G as the tonic of a G major scale. D is the fifth degree of the G major scale, making this interval a **perfect 5th**.

Example 2: D to C

To name this interval, think of D as the tonic of a D major scale. C# is the seventh degree of the D major scale (a major 7th). C is a semitone lower than C#, so this interval is a **minor 7th**.

Example 3: C# to E

To name this interval, if you do not know the key signature of C# major, think instead of the C major scale. E is the third degree of the C major scale – a major 3rd above C. C# is a semitone higher than C, so the interval is a **minor 3rd**.

Table of intervals

Compound intervals

All of the intervals mentioned so far have been of an octave or less and are sometimes called **simple intervals**. Intervals that are wider than an octave are known as **compound intervals**.

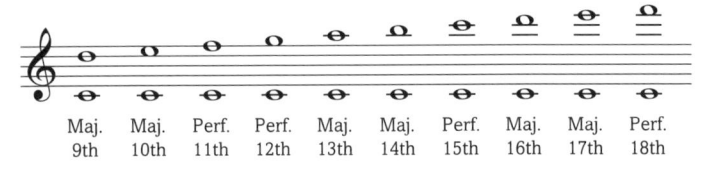

Compound intervals

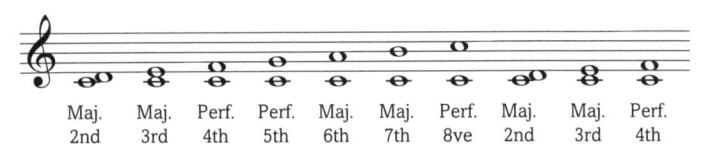

Corresponding simple intervals

Compound intervals keep the same qualities as the corresponding simple intervals. So a 9th from C to D is a major 9th, an 11th from C to F is a perfect 11th, and so on.

Naming compound intervals

Compound intervals can be numbered in two ways:

1 By including the octave as in the first example above: major 9th, major 10th, perfect 11th, and so on
2 By subtracting the octave(s) as in the second example above: compound major 2nd, compound major 3rd, compound perfect 4th, and so on.

> To calculate the number of a compound interval, subtract 7 from the larger number. For example, a perfect 12th is a compound perfect 5th (12 minus 7).

Enharmonic intervals

Some notes sound the same as each other but are written (or 'spelt') differently; these are said to be '**enharmonic**'. For example, the augmented 4th and the diminished 5th are enharmonic equivalents because the F♯ sounds the same as the G♭.

Aug. 4th   Dim. 5th

Consonant and dissonant intervals

Harmonic intervals can be classified as **consonant** or **dissonant**.

Dissonant intervals feel somewhat unstable, as though one of the notes needs to move up or down to resolve into a consonance. The major 7th, for example, feels as though it needs to resolve upwards, and the minor 7th feels as though it needs to resolve downwards.

Major 7th   Minor 7th

Major and minor 2nds, perfect 4ths, major and minor 7ths and all augmented and diminished intervals are **dissonant**.

Consonant intervals feel relatively stable and do not need to resolve to another interval. Major and minor 3rds and 6ths, perfect 5ths and octaves are all consonant intervals. Two voices producing exactly the same pitch are said to be in **unison**.

Table of intervals and music examples

Interval	Ascending/descending	Music example
Minor 2nd	ascending	*Ode to Joy* from Symphony No. 9 by Beethoven
Minor 2nd	descending	*Für Elise* by Beethoven
Major 2nd	ascending	*Eastenders* theme tune
Major 2nd	descending	*Yesterday* by the Beatles
Minor 3rd	ascending	*Greensleeves* (trad.)
Minor 3rd	descending	*Misty* by Erroll Garner
Major 3rd	ascending	*Morning has broken* (trad.)
Major 3rd	descending	*Summertime* by George Gershwin
Perfect 4th	ascending	*Amazing Grace* (trad.)
Perfect 4th	descending	*O come all ye faithful* (Christmas carol)
Tritone	ascending	*The Simpsons* theme tune by Danny Elfman
		Maria from *West Side Story* by Leonard Bernstein
Tritone	descending	*Close every door to me* from *Joseph* by Andrew Lloyd Webber

(continued)

Interval	Ascending/descending	Music example
Perfect 5th	ascending	*Also Sprach Zarathustra* by Richard Strauss
Perfect 5th	descending	*What shall we do with the drunken sailor?* (trad.)
Minor 6th	ascending	*Valse Op. 64 No. 2* by Chopin
Minor 6th	descending	*Love Story film theme* by Francis Lai
Major 6th	ascending	*Nocturne Op. 9 No. 2* by Chopin
Major 6th	descending	*Nobody knows the trouble I've seen* (African-American spirtual)
Minor 7th	ascending	*Somewhere* from *West Side Story* by Leonard Bernstein
Minor 7th	descending	*An American in Paris* by George Gershwin
Major 7th	ascending	*Somewhere over the rainbow* by Harold Arlen (notes 1 and 3)
Major 7th	descending	*I love you* by Cole Porter (notes 2 and 3)
Octave	ascending	*Somewhere over the rainbow* by Harold Arlen
Octave	descending	*There's no business like show business* by Irving Berlin (notes 2 and 3)

Theory in practice: recognising intervals – listening

Harmonic intervals
You can learn to recognise harmonic intervals by
- listening to the two notes and separating them
- listening for consonances and dissonances.

Melodic intervals
When identifying a melodic interval, you may find it helpful to:
- sing up a scale in your head, starting on the note of the lower interval, until you reach the upper note
- think of a melody that opens with that interval.

Scales

'Scales, and all their musical relations (arpeggios, broken chords and so on), are patterns of related pitches that we use to create melody (and to learn to control our instruments). Virtually every melody ever written, since about the sixteenth century, is based on scale patterns. They come in many different guises, each of which creates its own unique sound-world: from the basic major and minor scales found in Western music, to the evocative pentatonic scales and the more esoteric octatonic scale. Call any melody you like to mind, and you'll almost certainly find scale patterns. If you know your scales, you have a passport into a rich musical world.'

Paul Harris

Introducing scales

A **scale** is a pattern of notes arranged in order, from low to high (or vice versa).

Major and **minor** scales are known as **diatonic** scales and are built on patterns of seven notes within an octave span (see page 26). These patterns, which are built on a combination of **tones** and **semitones** (see below), give each kind of scale a characteristic sound.

The degrees of the scale

First degree	**Tonic**	Key-note
Second degree	**Supertonic**	The note above the tonic
Third degree	**Mediant**	The note midway between the tonic and the dominant
Fourth degree	**Subdominant**	The note below the dominant
Fifth degree	**Dominant**	Next in importance to the tonic
Sixth degree	**Submediant**	The note above the dominant
Seventh degree	**Leading note**	The note leading to the tonic

Tones and semitones

Tones and semitones are measurements of pitch. There are semitones between all adjacent notes on a keyboard, whether black or white. A tone consists of two semitones.

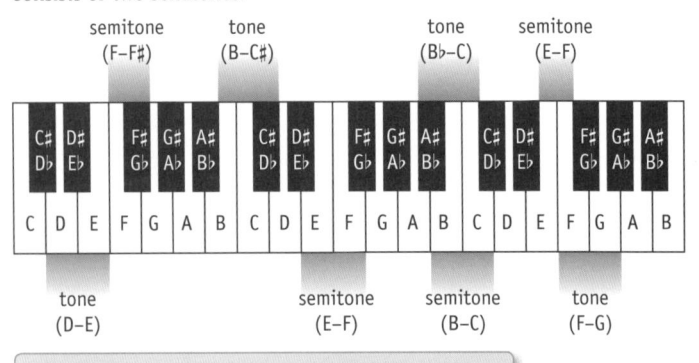

> There are two places in each octave where there is a semitone between two neighbouring white notes: B-C and E-F.

F   F♯   E♭   E (nat.)   B   C   E   F

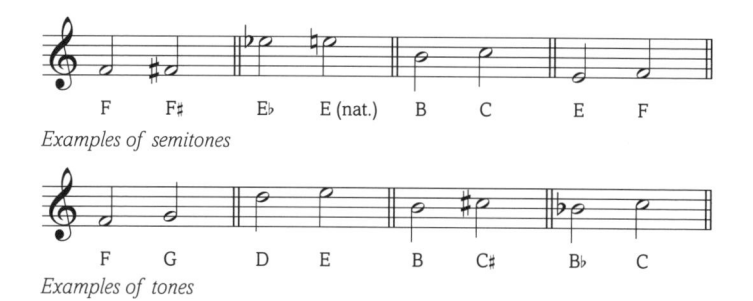

Examples of semitones

F   G   D   E   B   C♯   B♭   C

Examples of tones

Major scales

All major scales are built on the following pattern:

tone   tone   semitone   tone   tone   tone   semitone

The semitones come between the 3rd and 4th degrees of the scale and between the 7th degree and the octave.

Here is the scale of C major – it uses only the white notes on the keyboard:

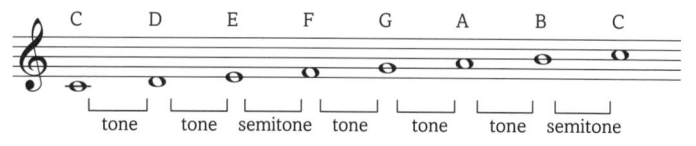

C   D   E   F   G   A   B   C

tone   tone   semitone   tone   tone   tone   semitone

> The major scale uses the same pattern of notes as the Ionian mode (see p.123 for the Table of Modes).

The major scale can be reproduced at any pitch, meaning that it can start on any note. Here is the scale of G major:

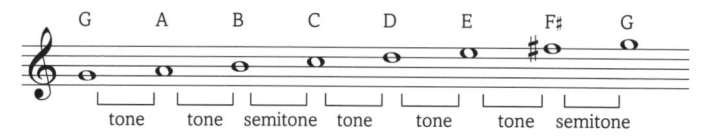

G   A   B   C   D   E   F♯   G

tone   tone   semitone   tone   tone   tone   semitone

Notice that an F♯ is needed in order to keep to the correct pattern of tones and semitones, i.e. so that there is a semitone between the leading note (F♯) and the tonic (G).

Here is the scale of F major:

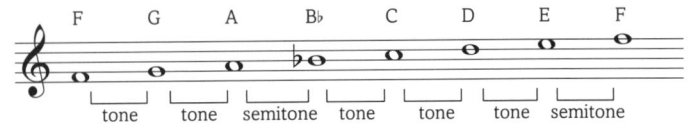

[Musical notation showing F major scale: F G A B♭ C D E F with intervals labeled: tone, tone, semitone, tone, tone, tone, semitone]

Notice that a B♭ is needed in order to keep to the correct pattern of tones and semitones.

Key signatures

When a piece of music is based on a particular scale, it is said to be in the key of that scale. For example, a work in the key of G major will use the notes found in the G major scale, meaning that F♯s rather than F♮s will be used throughout, unless otherwise indicated. Instead of writing a ♯ sign every time an F♯ is used, this is shown as a **key signature**:

Key signature for G major

The same principle applies to music in any key.

A key signature is positioned:
- at the beginning of *every* line of music
- *after* the clef
- *before* the time signature.

> Ledger lines are *never* used in a key signature.

Key signatures of the sharp major keys

[Musical notation showing key signatures for: C, G, D, A, E, B, F♯, C♯]

Notice that:
- the sharps always appear in the same order: F♯ C♯ G♯ D♯ A♯ E♯ (count *up* a 5th from the preceding one).
- the final sharp is the leading note of the key. For instance, the final sharp of E major is D♯.
- each new key is a 5th above the preceding one. For instance, A major has three sharps and E major (a 5th above) has four sharps.

Key signatures of the flat major keys

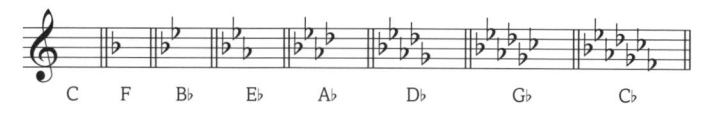

C F B♭ E♭ A♭ D♭ G♭ C♭

Notice that:

- the flats always appear in the same order: B♭ E♭ A♭ D♭ G♭ C♭ (count *down* a 5th from the preceding one).
- the penultimate flat is on the same note as the key. For instance, the penultimate flat of A♭ major is on A.
- each new key is a 5th below the preceding one. For instance, A♭ major has four flats and E♭ major (a 5th below) has three flats.

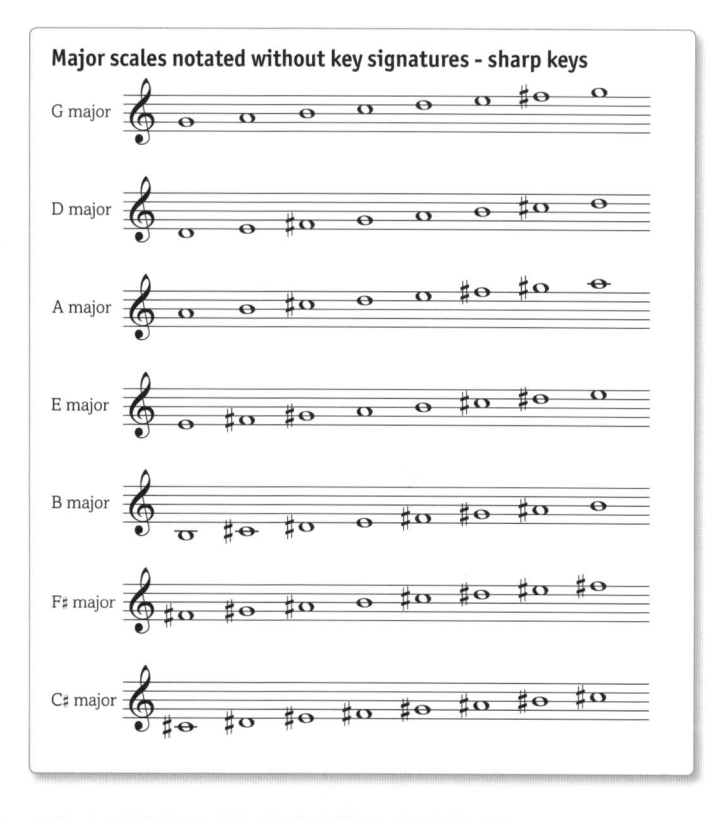

Major scales notated without key signatures - sharp keys

G major

D major

A major

E major

B major

F♯ major

C♯ major

Major scales notated without key signatures - flat keys

F major

B♭ major

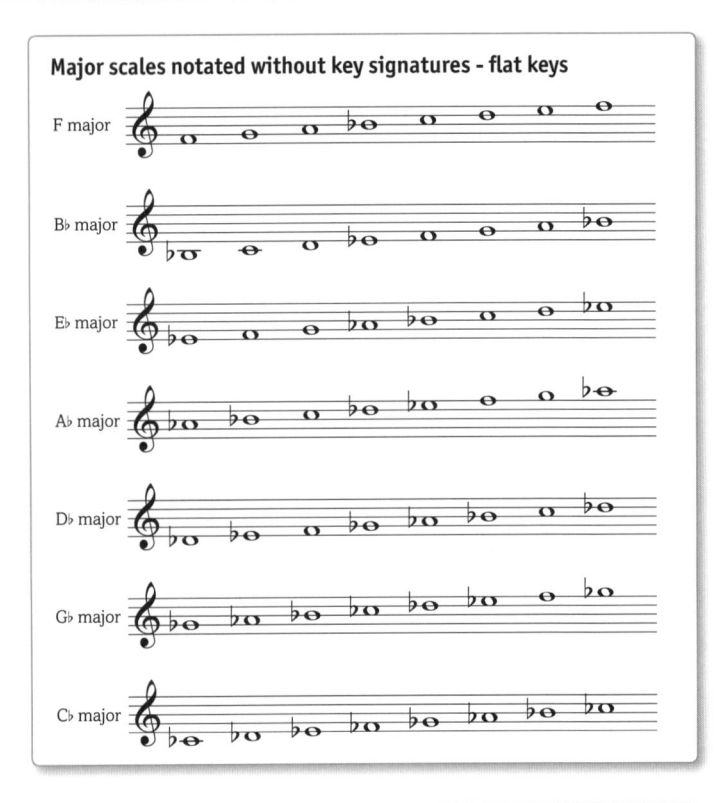

E♭ major

A♭ major

D♭ major

G♭ major

C♭ major

> C♯ major is the enharmonic equivalent of D♭ major (see page 24). Because D♭ major (five ♭s) has fewer accidentals than C♯ major (7♯s), composers usually choose the flat key. An exception is 'Ondine', the opening movement of Ravel's piano piece *Gaspard de la Nuit* (1908), which is in C♯ major.

Minor scales

There are three different versions of each minor key:

- the **natural** minor
- the **harmonic** minor
- the **melodic** minor

Each type of minor scale follows a different pattern of intervals, but always includes a minor 3rd between the tonic and the mediant. This minor 3rd helps to give the minor keys their characteristic sound.

Natural minor

All natural minor scales are built on the following pattern. The notes are the same, whether ascending or descending.

tone   semitone   tone   tone   semitone   tone   tone

The semitones come between the 2nd and 3rd, and the 5th and 6th degrees of the scale. This is the same sequence of tones and semitones given by the white notes of the piano, from A to A.

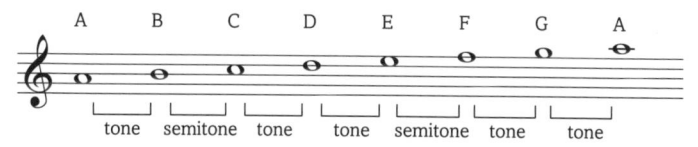

> The natural minor is found most often in pop music, folk and jazz. It uses the same pattern of notes as the Aeolian mode (see p.123 for the Table of Modes)

Here is the scale of C natural minor:

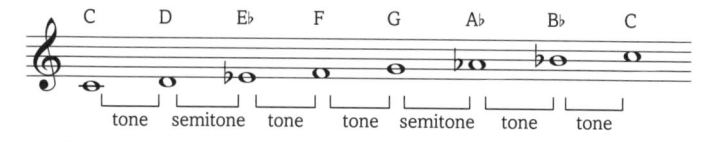

Notice that ♭s are needed on E, A and B in order to keep to the correct pattern of tones and semitones.

Harmonic minor

Harmonic minor scales are built on the following pattern. The notes are the same, whether ascending or descending.

tone   semitone   tone   tone   semitone   tone and a half   semitone

The semitones come between the 2nd and 3rd degrees of the scale and the 7th and octave. There is a tone and a half between the 6th and 7th degrees of the scale.

Here is the scale of A harmonic minor:

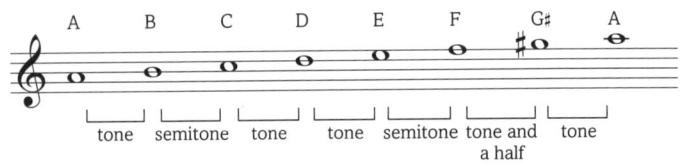

A – tone – B – semitone – C – tone – D – tone – E – semitone – F – tone and a half – G♯ – semitone – A

> The harmonic minor scale is so-called because it can be used to harmonise the three primary triads I, IV and V (see page 50).

Melodic minor

Melodic minor scales are built on the following pattern. Unlike the major, natural and harmonic minor scales, the pattern is different when ascending and descending.

Ascending:
tone   semitone   tone   tone   tone   tone   semitone

The semitones come between the 2nd and 3rd degrees of the scale and the 7th and octave.

Descending:
tone   tone   semitone   tone   tone   semitone   tone

The semitones come between the 2nd and 3rd degrees of the scale and the 5th and 6th.

Here is the scale of A melodic minor, ascending and descending.

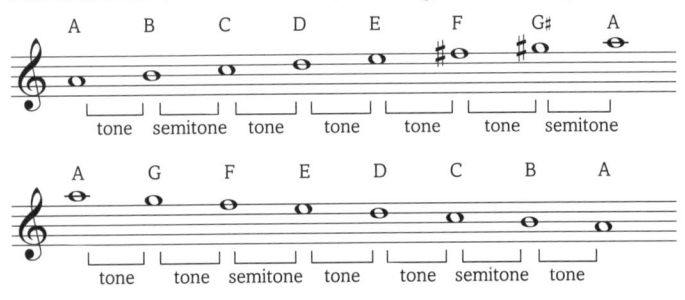

A – tone – B – semitone – C – tone – D – tone – E – tone – F♯ – tone – G♯ – semitone – A

A – tone – G – tone – F – semitone – E – tone – D – tone – C – semitone – B – tone – A

> The melodic minor does not include the leap of a tone and a half (augmented 2nd) – this enables a smoother melody line.

Relative major and minor keys

Major and minor keys with the same key signatures are said to be **related**. So:

- C major is the **relative major** of A minor.
- A minor is the **relative minor** of C major.

The key signature of a minor key is found by going up a tone and a half (a **minor 3rd**) from the tonic – this is the key-note of the relative major. So:

- The key signature of C minor is the same as the key signature of E♭ major.
- The key signature of D minor is the same as the key signature of F major.

Sharp keys			Flat keys		
C major	A minor		C major	A minor	
G major	E minor		F major	D minor	
D major	B minor		B♭ major	G minor	
A major	F♯ minor		E♭ major	C minor	
E major	C♯ minor		A♭ major	F minor	
B major	G♯ minor		D♭ major	B♭ minor	
F♯ major	D♯ minor		G♭ major	E♭ minor	
C♯ major	A♯ minor		C♭ major	A♭ minor	

Table of key signatures – major and minor

Tonic major and tonic minor

When a major and minor key both have the same key-note (tonic), one is said to be the **tonic major** or **tonic minor** of the other. So:

- C major is the **tonic major** of C minor.
- D minor is the **tonic minor** of D major.

The circle of fifths

The circle of fifths is a useful way of demonstrating the relationship between different keys.

- The **primary triads** (**I**, **IV** and **V** – see page 50) of any key can be found by looking on either side of the key-note (tonic). For instance, in the key of C, the two adjacent keys are G (**V** – the **dominant**) and F (**IV** – the **subdominant**).
- The three most closely related keys are the **dominant** (**V**), the **subdominant** (**IV**) and the **relative minor or major**. When a piece of music changes key (or **modulates**), it is most likely to move to one of these keys.
- Three of the major keys (B, F♯, and D♭) have two spellings each – B/C♭, D♭/C♯ and F♯/G♭. These are called **enharmonic notes** (see page 24). The equivalent minor keys can also be spelt in two ways.

The circle of fifths

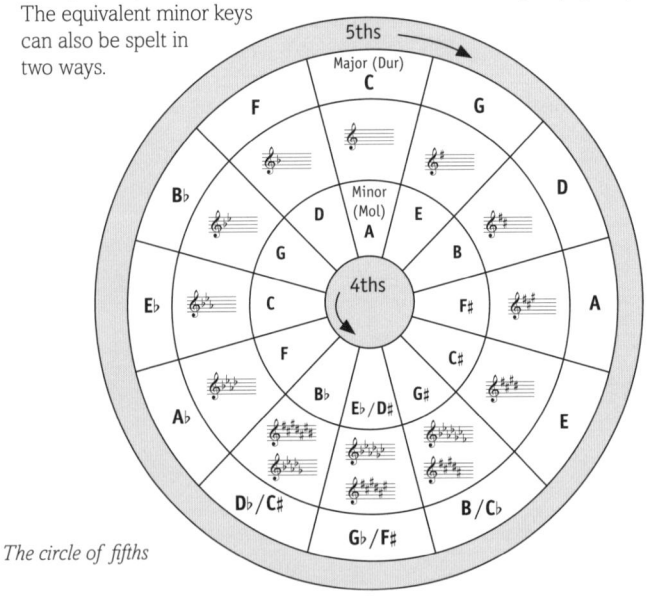

> **Theory in practice: identifying keys without a key signature**
> - Note down the accidentals used in the melody and write them in the order that they would appear in a key signature.
> - Identify the key signature.
> - Look at the melody again and decide whether it is in a major or minor key. If it is a minor key, you will probably find accidentals outside of the key signature, such as a sharpened leading note. The melody may also start or end on the key-note.
>
> **Example 1**
>
> Extract from *Sleep Song* by Humperdinck
>
> - There are two accidentals - F♯ and C♯.
> - There are sharps in the key signatures of D major and B minor.
> - There is no sharpened leading note (A♯), so the key must be D major.
>
> **Example 2**
>
> Extract from *Preludio* by Vivaldi
>
> - There are three accidentals – B♭, E♭ and F♯
> - There are two flats in the key signatures of B♭ major and G minor.
> - There is a sharpened leading note (F♯) so the key must be G minor.

Chromatic scales

The chromatic scale is made up of all the twelve notes in an octave and is formed entirely of semitones. It may begin on any note. There are several different ways of writing a chromatic scale, but you should always include the following:

- at least one and not more than two notes on each line and space
- the unaltered subdominant (IV) and dominant (V)
- the sharpened subdominant (IV).

There are various ways to write a chromatic scale. It does not matter which version you use – composers usually write whatever is most convenient. Here are four different forms of the chromatic scale starting on C:

1.

This is sometimes known as the **harmonic chromatic scale**. Each letter name appears twice, apart from the tonic and dominant.

2.

This is sometimes known as the **melodic (or arbitrary) chromatic scale (major)**. Each letter name appears twice, apart from the median and leading note.

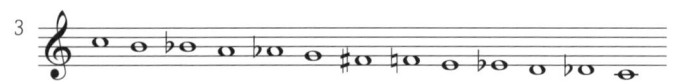

3.

This is the descending version of the harmonic and melodic chromatic scales. Each letter name appears twice, apart from the tonic and dominant.

4.

This is sometimes known as the **melodic (or arbitrary) chromatic (minor)**. Each letter name appears twice, apart from the median and dominant.

> The word 'chromatic' comes from 'chroma', the Greek word for *colour*. A chromatic scale is so named because it is formed from a diatonic scale with added chromatic notes adding colour.

Pentatonic scales

Pentatonic scales have five notes. The word 'pentatonic' comes from the Greek word 'pente', meaning five. They are very common in folk music from around the world and are a useful basis for improvising in jazz, pop, and rock music as they work well over several chords.

Pentatonic major

The pentatonic major uses the same notes as a major scale, but omits the 4th and 7th degrees:

Pentatonic scale on C

The notes of the pentatonic major scale correspond with the black notes of the keyboard starting on G♭:

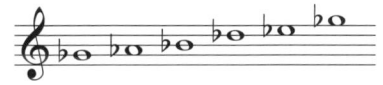

Pentatonic scale on G♭

> The song 'Amazing Grace' is based on the pentatonic major scale.

Pentatonic minor

The pentatonic minor uses the same notes as the natural minor scale, but omits the 2nd and 6th degrees:

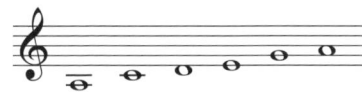

Pentatonic minor scale on A

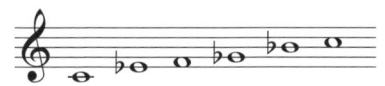

Pentatonic minor scale on C

The notes of the pentatonic minor scale correspond with the black notes of the keyboard starting on E♭:

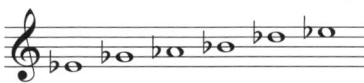

Pentatonic minor scale on E♭

> The French composers Debussy and Ravel both used pentatonic scales in some of their works. Debussy uses the pentatonic major scale in his piano piece, *La fille aux cheveux de lin* (The girl with the flaxen hair).

Whole-tone scale

The whole-tone scale is made up of six whole tones starting on either C or D♭ (its only transposition).

Whole-tone scale on C

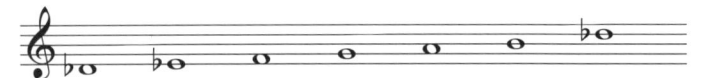

Whole-tone scale on D♭

> Debussy uses the whole-tone scale in his piano piece *Voiles* (Preludes, Book 1).

Octatonic scale

The octatonic scale is made up of eight notes alternating between tones and semitones:

> Stravinsky used the octatonic scale in his ballets *Petrushka* and *Rite of Spring*.

Harmony

'In the beginning there was rhythm. Then man began to sing, and there was melody. Eventually two voices sang together, and in that instant man created harmony. Whenever two or more lines of music sound together, we have harmony. So much of the emotional expression of Western music is caused by the tensions and resolutions set up between consonant and dissonant harmony.'

Paul Harris

Introducing chords and triads

The study of harmony centres on chords and their relationships to each other. A **chord** is the simultaneous sounding of two or more notes to produce harmony. Harmony is a fundamental element of Western music. The basic building block of harmony is the **triad**, a chord made up of three notes. The chord of C, for example, is made up of the notes C, E and G. C is the **root**, E is the **3rd**, because it is the third degree of the scale (counting up from the root) and G is the **5th**.

Tonic triads

The tonic triad is built on the tonic (or key-note) of a key. Here are the tonic triads of C, F, and G major. They are all major chords:

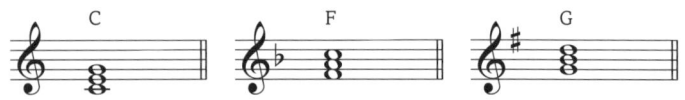

Here are the tonic triads of A, D and E minor. They are all minor chords:

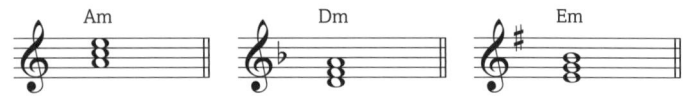

A triad can be formed on any degree of the scale (see page 26) and takes its name from that degree, e.g. dominant chord, tonic chord, and so on.

Major and minor triads

These are the two main kinds of triad. The major triad has a major 3rd from the root and the minor triad has a minor 3rd from the root. Both have perfect 5ths from the root.

major triad = root + major 3rd + perfect 5th
C major triad = *C* + *E* + *G*

minor triad = root + minor 3rd + perfect 5th
C minor triad = *C* + *E♭* + *G*

Primary and secondary triads

The triads built upon the tonic, subdominant and dominant degrees are known as the **primary triads**. The primary triads are the most frequently used chords in Western music and help to establish the key most strongly. Chords built on the other degrees of the scale are known as **secondary triads** (see page 26).

Below are the primary triads of C major. Each chord has a major 3rd and a perfect 5th from the root and is therefore a **major chord**:

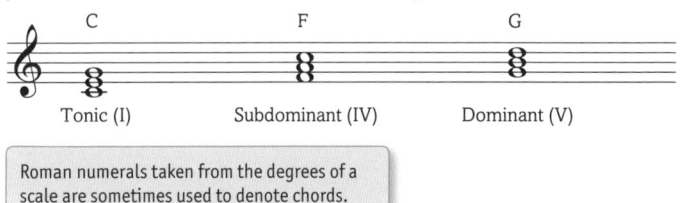

C — Tonic (I)
F — Subdominant (IV)
G — Dominant (V)

> Roman numerals taken from the degrees of a scale are sometimes used to denote chords.

Chords I and IV in a minor key have a minor 3rd and a perfect 5th from the root and are therefore **minor** chords. However, chord V in a minor key has a major 3rd and a perfect 5th from the root and is therefore a **major** chord. Here are the primary triads of A minor:

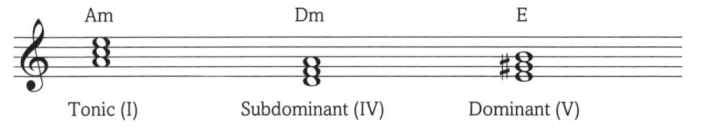

Am — Tonic (I)
Dm — Subdominant (IV)
E — Dominant (V)

> Notice the accidental on the 3rd in chord V (G#). This is used because it is the leading note in the harmonic minor scale (see page 40).

Major, minor, diminished and augmented chords

Triads are most frequently identified as one of four chord types: major, minor, diminished and augmented. They are made up of the following intervals:

major root = root + major 3rd + perfect 5th
minor root = root + minor 3rd + perfect 5th
diminished = root + minor 3rd + diminished 5th
augmented = root + major 3rd + augmented 5th

Here is an example of each type of chord built on C:

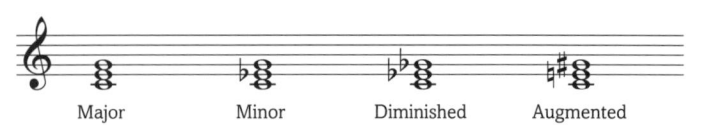

Major Minor Diminished Augmented

> You could also think of a triad as being built up by putting two 3rds on top of each other. The two types of 3rds (major and minor) can be combined in four different ways:
>
> 1 A minor 3rd placed over a major 3rd produces a major chord.
> 2 A major 3rd over a minor 3rd produces a minor chord.
> 3 A minor 3rd over a minor 3rd produces a diminished chord.
> 4 A major 3rd over a major 3rd produces an augmented chord.

When triads are built on each degree of the **major scale**, the following types of chord result:

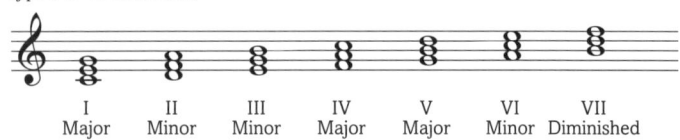

I	II	III	IV	V	VI	VII
Major	Minor	Minor	Major	Major	Minor	Diminished

When triads are built on each degree of the **minor scale**, the following types of chord result:

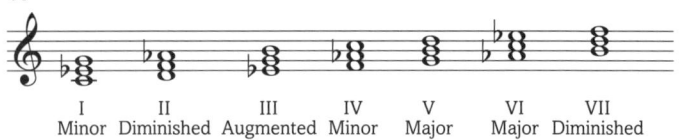

I	II	III	IV	V	VI	VII
Minor	Diminished	Augmented	Minor	Major	Major	Diminished

Seventh chords

Seventh chords are made by adding a 7th above the root on top of a triad. These are the seventh chords built on the different degrees of a C major scale:

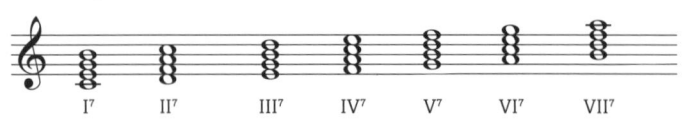

I^7 II^7 III^7 IV^7 V^7 VI^7 VII^7

These seventh chords can be categorised into four main types: the **dominant 7th**, the **major 7th**, the **minor 7th** and the **half-diminished 7th**.

Chord type	Degree of scale	Ingredients
Dominant 7th	V	a major chord + a minor 7th
Major 7th	I, IV	a major chord + a major 7th
Minor 7th	II, III, VI	a minor chord + a minor 7th
Half-diminished 7th	VII	a diminished chord + a minor 7th

The most common seventh chord is the dominant 7th.

Chords in root position

So far all of the chords have been shown with notes arranged by degree of the scale: with the root as the bass note (the lowest-sounding note), the 3rd above the root and the 5th above the 3rd. Chords built on the root of the scale, as these are, are known as chords in **root position**. Root position chords can also be arranged so that the relative positions of the 3rd and 5th are switched:

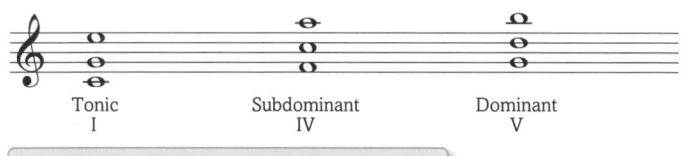

Tonic
I

Subdominant
IV

Dominant
V

The 3rd of each chord has been placed up one octave.

Doubling

When writing music for four voices, one of the notes in each triad must be doubled. There are conventions governing which notes to double in major and minor triads:
- In a major triad, the root or 5th is usually doubled but not the 3rd.
- In a minor triad, any note may be doubled.
- A chord may be written without the root or the 5th but not without the 3rd. The 3rd is important in giving the major or minor character of the chord.

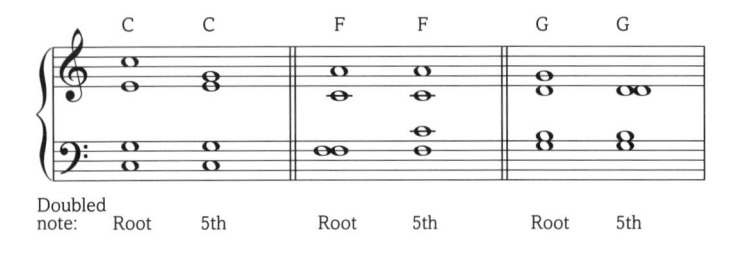

[Musical example showing C, C, F, F, G, G chords with doubled notes indicated below]

Doubled note: Root — 5th — Root — 5th — Root — 5th

Closed and open position

When a triad is arranged with all its notes close together, it is said to be in **closed position**:

Closed position

> Notes in a closed position triad are arranged within one octave span.

When a triad is arranged with its notes spaced out, it is said to be in **open position**:

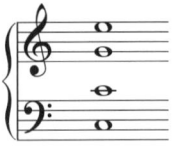

Open position

> Notes in an open position chord are arranged over more than one octave span.

Chord inversions

When a chord is arranged so that the bass note is *not* the root of the chord, it is said to be 'in inversion'. There are two bass notes in a triad in addition to the root – the 3rd and the 5th; this means that there are two inversions of triad chords.

- When the bass note is the root of the chord, it is said to be in **root position**:

I or Ia

- When the bass note is the 3rd of the chord, it is said to be in **first inversion**:

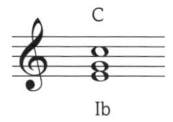

- When the bass note is the 5th of the chord, it is said to be in **second inversion**:

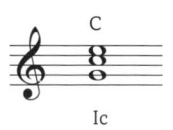

Seventh chords are made up of four notes, so they have three inversions. Here are the inversions of the dominant seventh chord (G7) in the key of C:

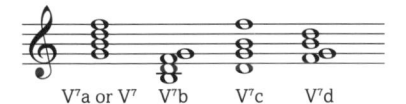

V⁷a or V⁷   V⁷b   V⁷c   V⁷d

> The 7th must not be doubled.

Naming chords

Roman numerals

Chords are commonly denoted using Roman numerals (I for the tonic, V for the dominant, etc., as in the examples above). It is possible to indicate the inversion of a chord when using Roman numerals in the following way:

- Root position chords can be shown either by Roman numeral alone (e.g. I, V) or with the letter 'a' placed after it (e.g. Ia, Va).
- First inversion chords are denoted by the letter 'b' placed after the Roman numeral (e.g. Ib, Vb).
- Second inversion chords are denoted by the letter 'c' after the Roman numeral (e.g. Ic, Vc).

Figured bass

An alternative way of indicating chord inversions is using **figured bass**, where a bass note is accompanied by a number (or 'figure') to indicate the required harmony. When chords are denoted by a figured bass, the intervals are counted up from the bass note:

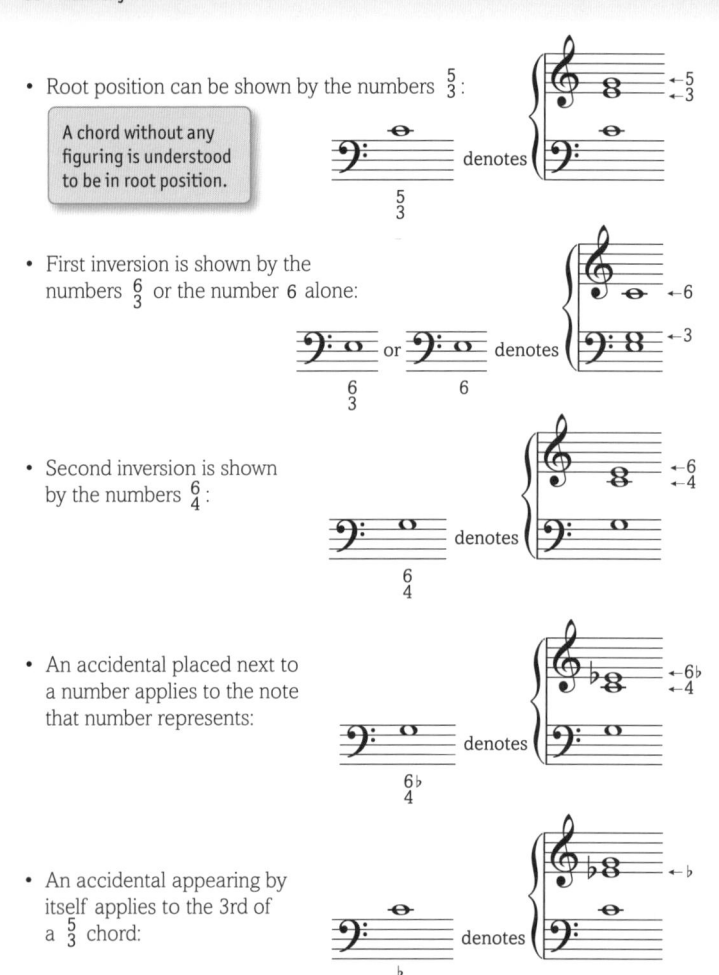

Harmony

- Root position can be shown by the numbers $\begin{smallmatrix}5\\3\end{smallmatrix}$:

  > A chord without any figuring is understood to be in root position.

  denotes $\leftarrow 5$ / $\leftarrow 3$

  (figure: $\begin{smallmatrix}5\\3\end{smallmatrix}$)

- First inversion is shown by the numbers $\begin{smallmatrix}6\\3\end{smallmatrix}$ or the number 6 alone:

  $\begin{smallmatrix}6\\3\end{smallmatrix}$ or 6 denotes $\leftarrow 6$ / $\leftarrow 3$

- Second inversion is shown by the numbers $\begin{smallmatrix}6\\4\end{smallmatrix}$:

  denotes $\leftarrow 6$ / $\leftarrow 4$

- An accidental placed next to a number applies to the note that number represents:

  $\begin{smallmatrix}6\flat\\4\end{smallmatrix}$ denotes $\leftarrow 6\flat$ / $\leftarrow 4$

- An accidental appearing by itself applies to the 3rd of a $\begin{smallmatrix}5\\3\end{smallmatrix}$ chord:

  $\flat$ denotes $\leftarrow \flat$

> The figured bass was used in the Baroque period: a bass instrument would play the given bass line while a keyboard or plucked instrument filled in the harmonies.

Pop and jazz chord notation

In pop and jazz music, chord names are often written above the stave. This shows the performer the essential notes of a chord around which they are free to improvise. Here is an example:

- The letter name of the root is shown by a capital letter, e.g. **C**
- The chord is assumed to be major unless otherwise indicated, e.g. **Am** (A minor), **Cdim** (C diminished)
- Numbers are added to indicate additional intervals from the bass note, e.g. **C7**
- A figure 7 alone implies a minor 7; a major 7th is written as 'maj7', e.g. **Cmaj7**
- Bass notes that are *not* the root of the chord can be indicated after the chord name, e.g. **F/A** indicates an F chord with A as the bass note.

Introducing cadences

Cadences are used to punctuate music, either bringing a melody to a point of repose before going on, or bringing it to a close. They are found at the end of musical phrases (see page 92) and serve a similar purpose to commas and full stops in a sentence. They are usually harmonised by two chords. The four main kinds of cadences are:

The **perfect cadence**	V–I
The **imperfect cadence**	Any chord followed by V (usually I–V, II–V or IV–V)
The **plagal cadence**	IV–I
The **interrupted cadence**	V followed by any chord (usually V–VI)

There are two cadences that end on the tonic chord: the perfect cadence and the plagal cadence. These cadences have the greatest sense of finality or completion.

The perfect cadence (V–I)

The perfect cadence (V–I) is frequently found at the end of pieces or sections of music. An example is the first movement of Beethoven's Symphony No. 5, which ends with eight perfect cadences played in succession. Another name for the perfect cadence is the **full close**.

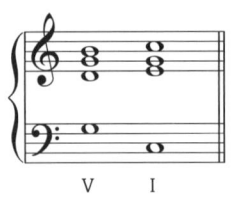

> The perfect cadence sometimes uses a dominant seventh (V7–I)

A perfect cadence in C major

The sense of finality in a perfect cadence comes from two things:
1 The move from the dominant (e.g. G) to the tonic or 'key-note' (e.g. C)
2 The leading note (e.g. B) rising to the tonic (e.g. C)

The imperfect cadence (I–V, II–V or IV–V)

The imperfect cadence always ends on the dominant chord. The dominant can be preceded by any other chord to create an imperfect cadence, but the most common progressions are I–V, II–V and IV–V. Imperfect cadences sound unfinished and give the impression that the music is going to continue. Another name for the imperfect cadence is the **half close**.

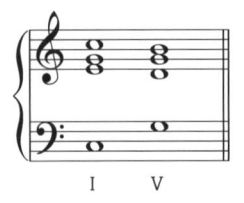

An imperfect cadence in C major

The plagal cadence (IV–I)

The plagal cadence consists of the subdominant chord followed by the tonic chord. Similar to the perfect cadence, it gives a sense of completion.

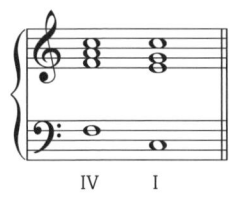

> Because the plagal cadence is often heard at the end of hymns on the word 'Amen', it is sometimes known as the 'Amen cadence'.

A plagal cadence in C major

The interrupted cadence (V–?)

The use of the dominant chord in an interrupted cadence leads the listener to expect a perfect cadence; however, instead of being followed by the expected tonic chord, another chord (often the submediant) is used. For this reason, the interrupted cadence is sometimes known as a **false close** or **surprise cadence**.

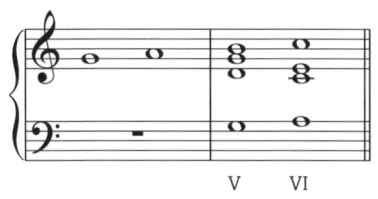

An interrupted cadence

The cadential $^6_4$–$^5_3$ chord progression

The cadential $^6_4$–$^5_3$ chord progression is often used to approach a perfect or an imperfect cadence:

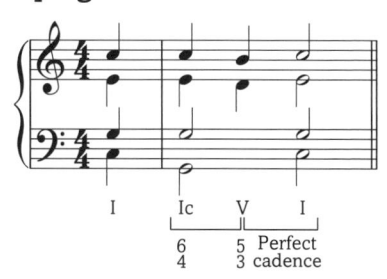

Harmonising notes

Melody and harmony are closely connected – each affects the shape of the other. Chords usually change less often than the notes of a melody – each chord is normally sustained over several notes. The rate at which chords change is known as **harmonic rhythm**: long-held chords and a slow rate of chord change can give a feeling of stasis, stillness or stability, whereas quicker changing chords can lend a sense of speed.

Chord layout and texture

The word **texture** refers to the different layers of sounds in music and how they are woven together. Rather than always being arranged in blocks, chords can be broken up or used as repeated phrases or **figurations** (see page 64); this is one way to vary the texture of a piece of music.

In his *Chaconne with 62 Variations* (1733), Handel treats the same chord sequence in a number of ways to produce different effects.

> A chaconne is a type of musical form in which a repeated chord sequence or bass pattern is used as the basis for variations.

Homophony

This is the basic chord sequence that Handel uses in his *Chaconne*:

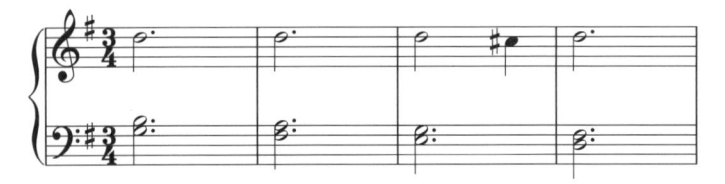

The texture of this chord sequence is **homophonic**. Homophonic music is played in block chords and literally means 'sounding together'. One part, usually the top part, has the melodic interest.

Polyphony

Polyphony literally means 'different sounds or voices' and refers to music made up of two or more melodic lines that weave in and out of one another.

> Another term for a polyphonic texture is 'contrapuntal'.

Canon

A canon is a contrapuntal device where a melody in one part is later repeated in another part. Handel uses the notes of the chords to form a canon in Variation 62:

Broken chords

A broken chord is a term for when the notes of a chord are sounded individually. In Variations 2 and 21 of the *Chaconne*, Handel uses different kinds of broken chords in the left hand:

> Here, the left-hand part is a quaver pattern based on the notes of each chord.

Variation 21

> Here, the right-hand line is decorated with passing notes while the left hand plays simple crotchet broken chords.

Variation 2

> ### Passing notes and auxiliary notes
>
> A passing note is a type of non-essential note found in melodies. Non-essential notes are decorative and do not form part of the harmony; instead they move stepwise from one harmony note towards another. A further type of non-essential note is the auxiliary note. Auxiliary notes are used to move stepwise between two repeated notes.

Arpeggios and the Alberti bass

Two commonly used types of broken chords that don't feature in Handel's *Chaconne* are arpeggios and the Alberti bass. In an **arpeggio**, the notes of a chord are played in order, from the lowest to the highest or vice versa:

> The word arpeggio comes from the Italian verb *arpeggiare*, meaning 'to play the harp'.

An **Alberti bass** is a left-hand keyboard figuration made up of broken triads whose notes are played in a specific order (low–high–middle–high). The Alberti bass is found in a great deal of piano music from the Classical period, such as the slow movement of Mozart's Piano Sonata in C, K. 545:

> The Alberti bass takes its name from the composer Domenico Alberti (c.1710–40) who used it frequently.

Scalic figuration

A figuration is a short musical phrase or embellishment that is often repeated. In Variation 38, Handel uses a scalic figuration:

Transposition

'Why transpose? The skill of transposition is highly undervalued and in fact has great benefits for all musicians. Being able to hear a melody, and then play or sing it starting on any given note, proves you have a deep understanding of its shape. You may even find it helps with your technical delivery.'

Paul Harris

Introducing transposition

Transposition is the process of writing or performing music at a higher or lower pitch than the given score. When a piece of music is transposed, all notes are raised or lowered by the same interval. Musicians are often called upon to write or perform music in keys other than the original. Transposition is used:

- when a piece or part needs to be performed on different instruments from those specified in the original score
- when a piece or part is written or played on a transposing instrument (see page 70)
- when a singer finds a melody in the original key too high or low for their vocal range.

> Songs are often published in alternative keys for 'high voice', 'middle voice' and 'low voice'.

Transposing at the octave

The most straightforward transposition is at the octave; this means transposing notes either up or down by the interval of an octave. With octave transposition, the note names, key signature and any accidentals remain the same as the original score:

Upper octave

Middle octave

Lower octave

A melody written at three different octaves

In the above example, the lowest octave transposition has been written in the bass clef; this means that the notes fit within the stave, making the music easier to read.

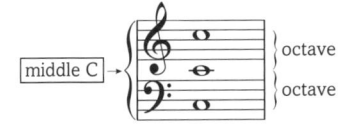

C written at three different octaves on a piano keyboard staff

Octave transposition into the alto or tenor clef

Although most music is written in either the treble or the bass clef, it is sometimes more appropriate to use the alto or tenor clef (see page 22). Both of these clefs have a range of notes falling between the ranges covered by the treble and bass clefs. Viola music, for example, is conventionally written in the alto clef because this is the best fit for the range of notes played on the instrument.

The relative position of middle C in each clef

J. S. Bach's unaccompanied cello suites are transposed up an octave and into the alto clef when they are played on the viola. Here is the opening of the 'Gigue' from Suite No. 2 in D minor:

Original cello music, written in the bass clef

The key and any accidentals remain the same as the original score.

Transposed for viola – the music has been transposed up an octave and written in the alto clef

Transposing into another key

When transposing music up or down by an interval other than an octave, the key signature of the music will change. The following passage from Beethoven's Symphony No. 8, III (1812) is in F major (with a key signature of one flat):

To transpose this passage up by a major 2nd, a key signature of G major (one sharp) is needed in order to produce the same pattern of intervals:

Similarly, in order to transpose this passage down by a perfect 5th, a key signature of B♭ major is needed:

> Any accidentals used against specific notes in the original score need to be reflected in the transposition. For instance, the B♮ in the original passage above becomes a C♯ or an E♮ in the transposed scores.

Theory in practice: transposing checklist
- Have you included the correct clef, key signature and time signature?
- Is your first note correct? When transposing at the octave, make sure you have written it at the new octave and not at the same pitch or two octaves lower or higher.
- Have you included all accidentals in the original score that were used outside of the key signature?
- Are the intervals between every note exactly the same as the original? Take particular care on notes with accidentals.
- If transposing between bass clef and treble clef, make sure the notes that were in spaces in the original score are now on the lines, and vice versa.

Theory in practice: transposing tips

Transposing into another key

Once you have established the key of the original score, count up or down from the key-note by the required interval to find the new key and key signature. Next, write down the first note – there are several ways to work out the notes that follow:

1 Transpose each of the original notes in turn by the required interval, e.g. when transposing up by a major 2nd:

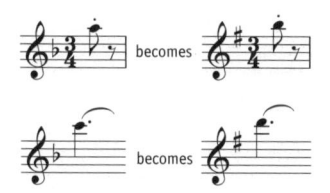

OR

2 Work out the degrees of the scale for each note in the original key, and then find equivalent notes in the new key:

Third degree

F major

Third degree

G major

OR

3 Follow the shape of the melody, imitating the pattern of intervals from one note to the next:

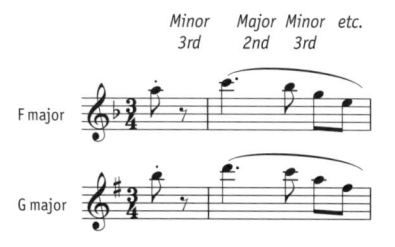

Minor Major Minor etc.
3rd   2nd   3rd

F major

G major

Transposing instruments

Transposing instruments are those instruments whose notes are written at a different pitch from how they sound. The pitch at which they *sound* is called **concert pitch**. In the following passage, all three instruments produce the melody at the same concert pitch, even though they are written differently:

> There are various reasons why transposing instruments are used, largely relating to making the music more straightforward for the performer to read and play. This was particularly the case for some instruments in their early stages of development.

The clarinet

The clarinet is a transposing instrument. The two most commonly used clarinets are the B♭ clarinet and the A clarinet. In the past, some composers wrote for a clarinet in C, but nowadays the slightly larger B♭ clarinet is preferred owing to its more mellow sound.

- A clarinet in B♭ is transposed up a major 2nd: when it plays a written C, a B♭ is sounded
- A clarinet in A is transposed up a minor 3rd: when it plays a written C, an A is sounded.

Having two clarinets enables players to avoid awkward keys, as they can select the instrument most appropriate for the music. For instance, a work in E major is easier to play on an A clarinet (written in the key of G major) than on the B♭ clarinet (where it would be written in F♯ major).

Octave transposition

When the range of an instrument is too high or too low for the music to be written clearly on bass or treble clef at the sounding octave, the music may be written an octave lower or higher to aid legibility.

- The piccolo, descant recorder and xylophone sound an octave higher than written.
- The double bass, guitar and contrabassoon sound an octave lower than written.
- The glockenspiel sounds two octaves higher than written.

Instrument	Written	Sounds	Key signature *(in order to sound in C major)*
Woodwind			
Cor anglais		Perfect 5th lower	G major
Clarinet in B♭		Major 2nd lower	D major
Clarinet in A		Minor 3rd lower	E♭ major
Clarinet in E♭		Minor 3rd higher	A major
Bass clarinet		Major 2nd plus an 8ve lower	D major
Soprano saxophone		Major 2nd lower	D major
Alto saxophone		Major 6th lower	A major
Tenor saxophone		Major 2nd plus an 8ve lower	D major
Baritone saxophone E♭		Minor 6th plus an 8ve lower	A major
Orchestral brass			
Horn in F		Perfect 5th lower	G major
Trumpet in B♭		Major 2nd lower	D major

Common transposing instruments

Transposing instruments in the brass band

The music for all of these brass band instruments is written in the treble clef; this means that players can switch between instruments more easily.

Instrument	Written	Sounds	Key signature *(in order to sound in C major)*
Soprano cornet		Minor 3rd higher	A major
Cornet		Major 2nd lower	D major
Flugelhorn		Major 2nd lower	D major
Tenor horn		Major 6th lower	A major
Baritone horn		Major 2nd lower	D major
Tenor trombone		Major 2nd lower	D major
Euphonium		Major 2nd plus an 8ve lower	D major
E♭ bass (tuba)		Major 6th plus an 8ve lower	A major
B♭ bass (tuba)		Major 2nd plus an 8ve lower	D major

Brass band transposing instruments

Instruments and voices

'In addition to the three basic elements of music – rhythm, melody and harmony – we have a multitude of instruments and voices that each has an individual sound-quality. Used in combination, instruments and voices offer an infinite kaleidoscope of sonic possibility.'

Paul Harris

Instruments of the orchestra

Orchestral instruments can be grouped into **woodwind**, **brass**, **percussion** and **strings**; together, these make up the four sections of the orchestra. Orchestral scores are organised accordingly, with instruments grouped by section and then usually arranged in order of pitch – from the highest sounding down to the lowest. Additional parts, such as a choir or a soloist, are placed immediately above the string section.

The opening bars of Beethoven's Symphony No. 8 are shown opposite.

Woodwind

Woodwind instruments are so called because originally they were made out of wood. Nowadays, however, they may be made out of wood, metal or synthetic materials.

Sound production

Sound is produced by causing a column of air to vibrate inside a hollow tube.

- The **flute** and **piccolo** are held horizontally. A stream of air is directed against the edge of the mouthpiece, an open hole, which sets up vibrations in the air column.

- The **clarinet** uses a **single reed** – a thin flat piece of cane attached to the mouthpiece. The player's breath causes the reed to vibrate, which in turn sets the air column vibrating.

- The **oboe**, **cor anglais** and **bassoon** use a double reed – two thin pieces of cane bound together. The two reeds vibrate against each other and set the air column vibrating.

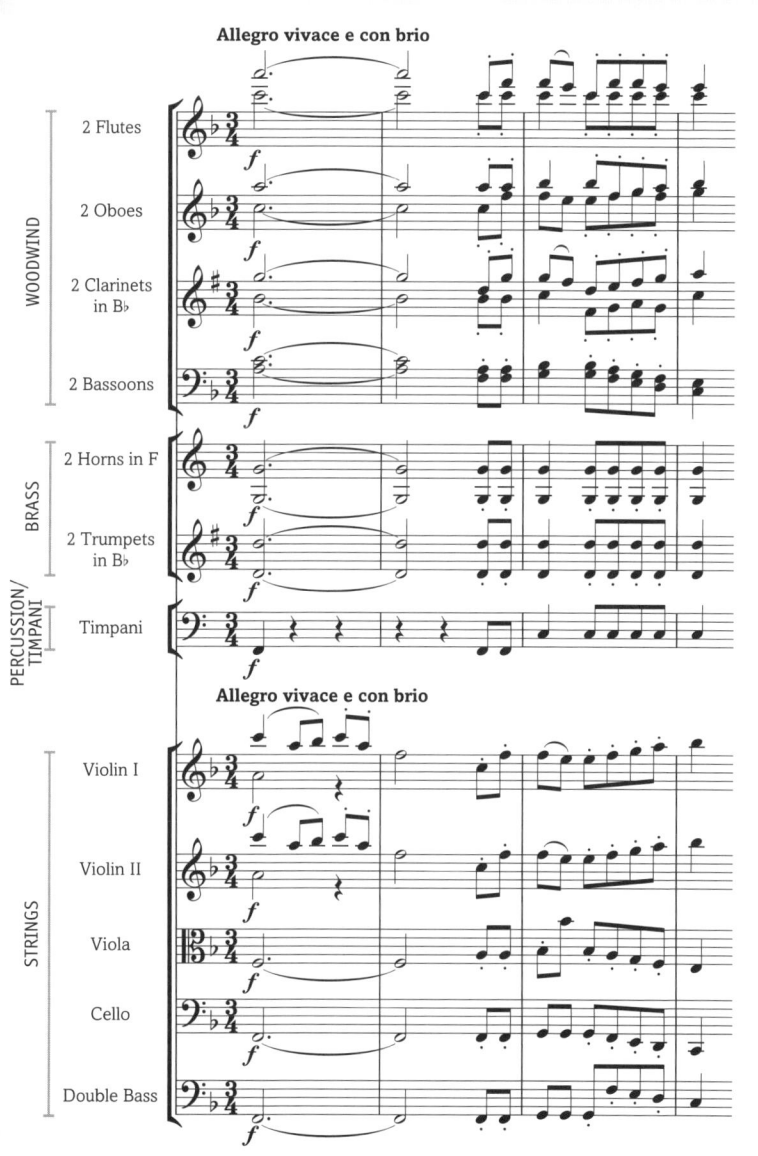

Extract from Symphony No. 8, Op. 93 (1812) by Beethoven

Ranges

Here is the written range of each of the standard orchestral woodwind instruments. Professional players will be able to play the full range of notes but when you are writing for these instruments you should usually avoid the extreme registers and stay within the range of the first two semibreves.

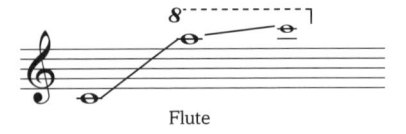

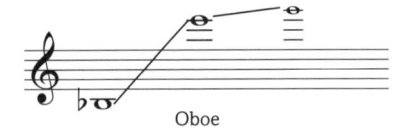

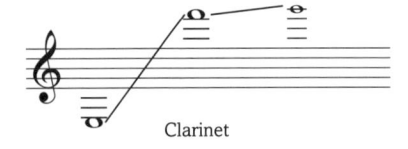

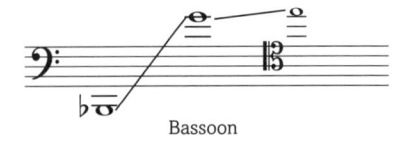

Flute

Oboe

Clarinet

Bassoon

Instrument*	Italian name	Clef used	Transposing instrument
Piccolo	Flauto piccolo	𝄞	Yes – sounds an octave higher than written
Flute†	Flauto	𝄞	No
Oboe†	Oboe	𝄞	No
Cor anglais	Corno inglese	𝄞	Yes – sounds a perfect 5th lower than written
Clarinet in E♭	Clarinetto	𝄞	Yes – sounds a minor 3rd higher than written
Clarinet in B♭†	Clarinetto	𝄞	Yes – sounds a major 2nd lower than written
Clarinet in A†	Clarinetto	𝄞	Yes – sounds a minor 3rd lower than written
Bass clarinet in B♭	Clarinetto basso	𝄞	Yes – sounds a major 9th lower than written
Bassoon†	Fagotto	𝄢 (𝄡 tnr)	No
Contrabassoon	Contrafagotto	𝄢	Yes – sounds an octave lower than written

Woodwind instruments

* The standard woodwind instruments found in the orchestra are indicated by a † and arranged in order of pitch, from highest to lowest.

Brass

All brass instruments are made out of metal. Nowadays however, they are more likely to be made out of mixed metals than pure brass. The table below (page 79) shows the order in which brass instruments are arranged in an orchestral score; note that the French horn is placed above the trumpet in spite of having a lower pitch range.

Sound production

Each brass instrument has a cup-shaped mouthpiece, a length of hollow tubing and a flared bell. The sound is produced by causing a column of air to vibrate inside a hollow tube. The vibrations are set up by the player's lips vibrating against the mouthpiece. Several notes can be sounded by the player simply by altering the tension of their lips: the tighter the lips, the higher the pitch. To obtain more notes, either **valves** or a **slide** are used to alter the length of the tube. Both work on the same principle: the longer the tube, the lower the note.

- The **French horn**, **trumpet** and **tuba** are all **valve** instruments. Each of the three valves brings into action an extra length of tubing and can be used in combination with each other to produce different pitches. When a valve is pressed down, an extra loop of tubing is added.

- The **trombone** and the **bass trombone** are both **slide** instruments. The slide works by lengthening or shortening the instrument's tube.

Brass instruments may be played with a **mute**: a device, usually made out of metal or wood, that is inserted in the bell and alters the quality of the sound. Mutes come in different shapes and sizes, each producing a different distinctive *timbre*. The following performance directions are used:

con sordini (or *con sord.*)   play with mute

senza sordini (or *senza sord.*)   play without mute

Ranges

The written range of each of the standard orchestral brass instruments is shown overleaf. Some players may be able to play higher or lower than the notes given, but when you are writing for these instruments you should usually avoid the extreme registers.

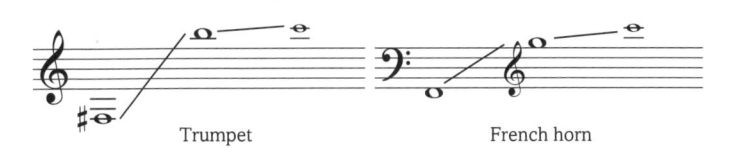

[Musical staves showing ranges for: Trumpet, French horn, Tenor trombone, Bass trombone, Tuba]

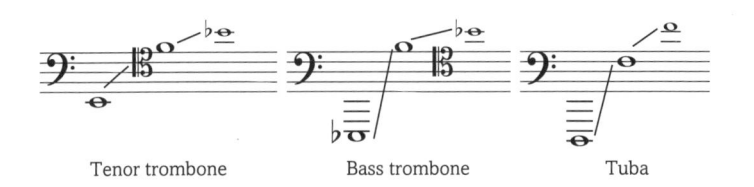

Instrument	Italian name	Clef used	Transposing?
French horn in F	Corno	𝄞 (𝄢)	Yes – sounds a perfect 5th lower than written
Trumpet in C	Tromba	𝄞	No
Trumpet in B♭	Tromba	𝄞	Yes – sounds a major 2nd lower than written
Tenor trombone	Trombone	𝄢 (𝄡 tnr)	No
Bass trombone	Trombone basso	𝄢	No
Tuba	Tuba	𝄢	No

Brass instruments

Percussion

Percussion instruments can be divided into two groups – those that are **pitched** or **tuned** and those that are **unpitched** or **untuned**. Pitched instruments can play notes of definite pitch and are capable of producing a melody (e.g. the xylophone or glockenspiel). Unpitched instruments play notes of indefinite pitch and can therefore only play rhythms (e.g. the bass drum).

In early orchestral music from the seventeenth and eighteenth centuries, percussion parts were often limited to timpani (or 'kettle drums'). Since the nineteenth century, however, percussion sections have become much larger and include a wide variety of sounds from this large and diverse family of instruments. For instance, *Turangalîla Symphonie* (1948) by the French composer Olivier Messiaen uses a huge percussion section that requires ten percussionists playing drums, vibraphone, glockenspiel, tubular bells, cymbals, maracas, tambourine, tam-tam, temple blocks, triangle and wood block.

Sound production

The percussion section is made up of instruments that produce sound vibrations by being struck, shaken or rubbed. Sticks and mallets (or 'beaters') are used to strike many percussion instruments; they come in a range of sizes with different types of heads made from materials such as rubber, felt or wood.

- The **timpani** and **bass drum** are played with mallets.
- The **side drum** is played with wooden sticks.
- **Cymbals** can be played in several ways: pairs of cymbals can be clashed, swished or rubbed together; a suspended cymbal can be struck.
- The **xylophone** and **glockenspiel** are struck with mallets.
- The **tubular bells** are struck with leather or plastic-headed hammers.
- The **tambourine** can be struck, shaken or rubbed to produce different sounds.
- The **triangle** is struck with a metal beater.

Tuned percussion ranges

Here is the written range of each of the standard tuned percussion instruments:

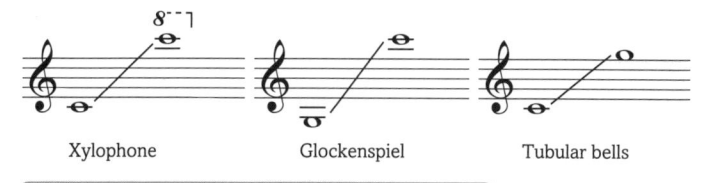

Xylophone — Glockenspiel — Tubular bells

> The glockenspiel sounds two octaves higher than notated.

Timpani can be tuned to a definite pitch by means of a foot pedal that tightens the head. They come in pairs of different sizes.

Timpani 38"   28"   25"   23"   21"

Instrument	Italian name	Clef used	Transposing?
Timpani (kettle drums)	Timpani	𝄢	No
Triangle	Triangolo	Unpitched	No
Cymbal	Piatti, Cinelli	Unpitched	No
Bass drum	Gran cassa	Unpitched	No
Snare (side) drum	Tamburo militare	Unpitched	No
Tambourine	Tamburo basco, Tamburino	Unpitched	No
Tubular bells	Campane, Campanelle	𝄞	No
Glockenspiel	Campanette, Campanelli	𝄞	Yes – sounds two octaves higher than written
Xylophone	Silofono	𝄞	Yes – sounds one octave higher than written

Tuned percussion instruments

Strings

The string section forms the basis of the orchestra, with over half of the performers playing a stringed instrument. Early orchestras in the seventeenth and eighteenth centuries were quite small, comprising around twenty string players and few other instrumentalists. Over time, more instruments and a larger numbers of string players were added to this ensemble, with around fifty string players being commonplace by the nineteenth century. In orchestral scores, stringed instruments are arranged in order of pitch, from highest to lowest.

Sound production

The sound of the orchestral stringed instruments is produced in the same way – four strings are stretched across a hollow wooden body and are made to vibrate by drawing a bow across them. They all work on the same principle – the shorter the string, the higher the note. The length of a string is made shorter by the player pressing it down with his fingers – this is called stopping. Double stopping is when two (or more) strings are played at the same time (see the score of Beethoven's Symphony No. 8 on page 75 for an example of violin double stopping).

Ranges

Here is the written range of each of the standard orchestral string instruments. Some players may be able to play higher than the highest note given, but when you are writing for these instruments you should usually avoid the extreme registers.

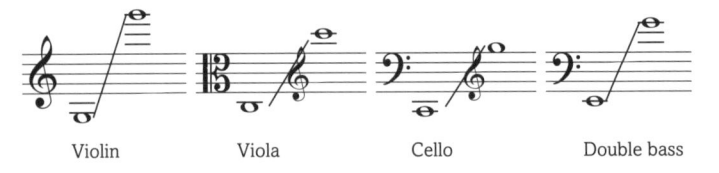

Violin   Viola   Cello   Double bass

> Many professional double bass players use a C extension, which extends the fingerboard under the lowest string and gives an additional four semitones. The lowest string is usually tuned down to C. Some players use a five-string bass which extends the lower range down to B.

Instrument	Italian name	Clef used	Transposing?
Violin	Violino	𝄞	No
Viola	Viola	𝄡 (𝄞)	No
Cello	Violoncello	𝄢 (𝄡 or 𝄞)	No
Double bass	Contrabasso	𝄢	Yes – sounds an octave lower than written

String instruments

Performance directions and techniques for stringed instruments

pizzicato plucked with the fingers

arco play with the bow (a direction following a *pizzicato* passage)

sul G play on the G string, *sul A* play on the A string etc.

sul ponticello play near the bridge

⌒ play in one stroke of the bow (either up or down)

⊓ play with a 'down' bow

∨ play with an 'up' bow

con sordini (or con sord.) with mute

senza sordini (or senza sord.) without mute

double stopping two strings are played at the same time

col legno turn the bow upside down and play with the wood on the strings

tremolo play with a rapid up-and-down movements of the bow to produce a quivering effect

Early keyboard instruments

Two of the most popular early keyboard instruments during the Renaissance and Baroque periods were the **harpsichord** and the **clavichord**.

> The Fitzwilliam Virginal Book is a collection of sixteenth- and seventeenth-century keyboard pieces intended to be played on the 'clavier' – a blanket term for keyboard instruments of the time, including virginals, harpsichord, clavichord and organ.

Harpsichord

The harpsichord was used extensively by such composers as J. S. Bach, Couperin, Handel and Domenico Scarlatti. The latter two composers, both born in 1685, composed a huge amount of music specifically for harpsichord: Scarlatti penned well over 500 sonatas for the instrument and Handel wrote numerous harpsichord suites, fugues and variations.

Sound production
- The sound of the harpsichord is produced by plucking strings. When a key is pressed down on the keyboard (or 'manual'), a strip of wood called a 'jack' rises up, enabling a plectrum to pluck the string.
- The same dynamic level results whatever pressure is applied to the keys.
- Some harpsichords have more than one manual.
- The largest harpsichords have a range of just over five octaves; the smallest have a range of under four octaves.

Clavichord

The clavichord was in common usage from the fifteenth to the eighteenth century. Because of its delicate sound, it was largely played at home and was regarded primarily as a teaching and practising instrument.

Sound production
- The sound of the clavichord is produced by hammering strings. When a key is pressed down, small brass blades called 'tangents' hit the strings.
- Although a comparatively small, quiet keyboard instrument, the clavichord is capable of producing different dynamics by varying the pressure applied to the keys.
- Clavichords vary in size, but most have a range of four-and-a-half or five octaves.

The piano

The pianoforte (or 'piano') was invented around 1700 by an Italian instrument maker called Bartolomeo Cristofori and has held a central place in the repertoire of Western music ever since. Cristofori called his new instrument the *gravicembalo col piano e forte*, with reference to the fact that, unlike the harpsichord, it could play with different dynamics. Pianos vary in size and have a range of up to seven and a half octaves.

Sound production

The sound of the piano is produced by hammering strings. When a key is pressed down, a felt-covered hammer hits the string; when it is released, a felt-covered damper is lowered to silence the sound.

The piano includes pedals that enable the player to vary the kind of sound produced. The **sustaining pedal** (on the right) works by lifting the damper, allowing the string to vibrate until the pedal is released. The **soft pedal** (on the left) is used to produce a more muted tone.

> **Performance directions for using the sustaining and soft pedals**
>
> *una corda* press the soft pedal
>
> *tre corde* release the soft pedal
>
> *con Ped.* play the passage with the sustaining pedal
>
> ℘ed. press the sustaining pedal
>
> ✽ release the sustaining pedal
>
> ℘ed.⎯⎯ press/release the sustaining pedal

> The American composer John Cage wrote many pieces for 'prepared piano', where new sounds are produced by inserting pieces of metal and wood between the strings.

Organ

The organ in its various forms has featured in Western music for centuries. The pipe organ rose in prominence during the Renaissance and Baroque periods and was extensively used by key composers of the time, including J. S. Bach.

Sound production

The sound of the organ is produced by wind passing through sets of pipes. The sets of pipes (or 'ranks') vary in size, with each rank producing a different *timbre* of sound (see page 73). Most organs have two or more manuals (keyboards) as well as pedals that are operated by the player's feet. This allows players to produce a large number of notes and timbres across the manuals and pedals.

- The sound of a **flue pipe** is produced by the air column vibrating (using the same principle as the flute).
- The sound of a **reed pipe** is produced by a vibrating reed (using the same principle as an oboe).
- Pipe organs range in size: a large modern organ has three or four manuals with five octaves each, and a two-and-a-half octave pedal board.

Orchestral ensembles

There are three main types of orchestra. The **symphony orchestra** is the largest, with around eighty to 100 members. It includes the widest range of instruments and is capable of playing the larger orchestral works of the nineteenth century and beyond. This includes symphonic repertoire by composers such as Brahms and Mahler as well as other orchestral repertoire in the form of overtures, concertos and tone poems.

The **chamber orchestra** usually has around fifty members or fewer and includes a smaller number of instruments. It is used for smaller-scale orchestral repertoire, such as the Classical symphonies by Mozart and Haydn and the Baroque concertos by J. S. Bach.

The **string orchestra** is made up of stringed instruments and sometimes percussion. It usually plays works specially written for strings alone, such as Mozart's *Eine Kleine Nachtmusik* and Bartók's *Divertimento for String Orchestra*.

Wind and brass bands

The **wind band** (or concert band) is made up of woodwind, brass and percussion instruments. The repertoire includes arrangements of film music and orchestral works, as well as specially written music such as the *English Folk Song Suite* by Vaughan Williams.

The **military band** is a wind band specialising in performing music for military functions. Its repertoire includes ceremonial and marching music.

The **brass band** is made up of brass and percussion instruments. Its repertoire is wide and includes marches and hymn tunes, arrangements of film music and orchestral works, as well as specially written works. Notable composers for brass band include Elgar Howarth, Malcolm Arnold and Harrison Birtwistle.

Chamber groups

Chamber music is composed for a small group of solo musicians – up to about ten players. It uses one player per part and is performed without a conductor. Some of the more common chamber music combinations are duets (two players), trios (three players), quartets (four players) and quintets (five players).

> The term 'chamber' comes from the word for a room, with reference to the fact that chamber music would traditionally be played in a room rather than a large concert hall.

Trios

A **string trio** is made up of three string instruments, often violin, viola and cello. A **piano trio** is made up of piano, violin and cello. Beethoven's 'Archduke' Trio Op. 97 (1811) is written for this combination.

Quartets and quintets

The **string quartet** is the most important type of composition for chamber group. A string quartet has two violins, a viola and a cello. Haydn was the first well-known composer to write string quartets in the eighteenth century, but it has maintained its popularity ever since, with leading composers such as Mozart, Beethoven and Bartók composing extensively for the ensemble.

> Stockhausen's *Helicopter String Quartet* (1993) was composed for 'four string players in four helicopters flying in the air and playing'.

The **string quintet** is made up of the string quartet instruments plus an extra viola, cello or double bass. One of the most famous string quintets is Schubert's String Quintet in C D956 (1828), which has two cellos.

The **wind quintet** is made up of flute, oboe, clarinet, French horn and bassoon. Notable works for wind quintet include Ligeti's *Six Bagatelles for Wind Quintet* (1953).

Vocal ensembles

A **choir** (sometimes known as a chorus) is an ensemble of singers. Some choirs belong to a church or cathedral; others perform in theatres and concert halls. Choirs are usually led by a conductor or choirmaster and are often accompanied by a piano, organ, or occasionally orchestra. The term 'a cappella' refers to unaccompanied choral singing.

> Thomas Tallis's motet *Spem in Alium* (*c.*1570) was written in forty parts for eight five-voice choirs.

Sound production

The sound of the voice is produced by air being expelled from the lungs and vibrating the vocal cords – the tighter the vocal cords, the higher the note. The cavities in the throat, mouth, nose and head act as resonators to amplify and colour the sound.

Vocal ranges

Here is the range of each of the standard voice-types found in choral music. Some singers may be able to sing higher or lower than the given notes, but when you are writing for these voices you should usually avoid the extreme registers.

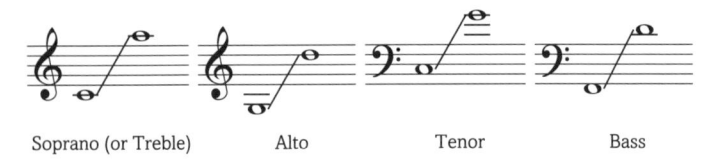

Soprano (or Treble)   Alto   Tenor   Bass

> Boys' voices that sit within the soprano range are known as 'trebles'.

Common choir scorings

- The most common type of vocal ensemble is the **mixed choir**. It is made up of sopranos, altos, tenors and basses (SATB), usually with more than one singer to a part.
- The **male-voice choir** is made up of men's voices, usually in up to four parts (TTBB scoring). Sometimes choirs comprising boys' and men's voices are described as male-voice choirs.

Instruments and voices

- The **upper-voice choir** is made up of female and/or boys' voices. Upper-voice music is usually scored for between two and four parts covering the soprano/treble and alto voice ranges (SA, SSA, SSAA).

Choral notation

There are a number of ways that choral music can be presented, depending on the complexity of the music and the relationship between the individual choral lines.

Open score

When each voice has a separate stave, the music is said to be written in **open score**. The parts are arranged in order of range, from highest at the top to lowest at the bottom. Lyrics are usually placed beneath each line, with dynamics and other instructions placed above:

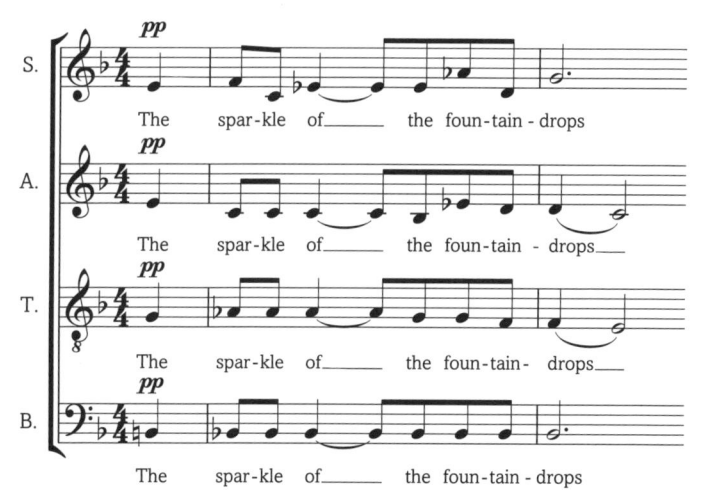

Extract from Dream tryst *(1902) by Gustav Holst*

> Open score is particularly useful in polyphonic music (see page 61), where the choral lines are rhythmically independent.

In open score, the tenor line is written in the treble clef because this fits well with the tenor's range of notes. However, the sounding pitch of the tenor line is an octave lower than its written pitch in the treble clef; this is indicated by the addition of an '8' to the standard clef sign:

Short score

When more than one voice is found on a stave, the music is said to be written in short score. Like open score, the parts are arranged from high to low. It is usual in short score for all of the voices to share the same line of lyrics, placed between the staves, and for dynamics to be placed above and below the staves.

Extract from Dream tryst *(1902) by Gustav Holst*

> Short score is often used when all parts sing the same words and syllables on the same beats.

Because the tenor part shares a stave with the bass part in short score, it is now written in bass clef, at sounding pitch.

Theory in practice: writing in short score
- The stems of the soprano and tenor parts always go up. The stems of the alto and bass parts always go down.
- When two parts on one stave sing a semibreve at the same pitch, two adjacent semibreves should be written:
- When two parts on the same stave have the same accidental, the accidental should be written separately for each part. In the extract above, the ♭ sign is placed against the E flat twice within a single bar, first for the soprano line on the second beat, and then for the alto line on the fourth beat.

Working with rhythm, melody and words

'The earliest form of melodic music was song; indeed for most of us, in our cradles, song was probably our first musical experience. All words have rhythm, and the transition from speech to song is actually a very natural one. Spend a day singing what you'd normally just say – you'll soon get a feel for word setting!'

Paul Harris

Phrases and structure

Broadly speaking, the structure of any piece of music relies on achieving a balance between repetition and contrast – this principle is important in the construction of phrases. **Phrases** are the melodic or rhythmic segments that, when combined, form the basis of musical works. They are usually made up of an even number of bars (often two, four or eight bars); phrases made up of an uneven number of bars are less common.

> Until the twentieth century, much of Western classical music was created around balanced four-bar phrases, where the second two bars would 'answer' the first two bars.

Developing rhythmic ideas

There are many ways in which phrases can be constructed and developed using rhythmic repetition, varied repetition and contrast. In his keyboard piece *The King's Hunt*, John Bull employs the same rhythm in bars 2 and 3 of this four-bar phrase:

Extract from The King's Hunt *by John Bull (1562–1628)*

In *Buffons* for Renaissance guitar, the composer Guillaime de Morlaye uses the same rhythm in bars 2 and 4:

Extract from Buffons *(1732) by Guillaime de Morlaye (c.1510–58)*

There are also many examples where composers repeat the rhythm of the first two bars in the third and fourth bars:

Allegro leggierissimo

Extract from Octet *in E♭ Op. 20, III (1825) by Mendelssohn*

Sometimes composers use different rhythms in each bar of a phrase:

Allegro

Extract from the 'London' Symphony (No. 104, I) (1795) by Haydn

---

Theory in practice: writing an answering phrase

An **answering phrase** follows on from an opening phrase as a kind of musical response or 'answer'. It usually shares similar characteristics to the opening phrase but is rarely identical.

When writing your own answering phrase, it will help to follow these general guidelines:

- Make your phrase the same length as the opening phrase.
- Tap out the rhythm of the opening phrase, or imagine how it sounds.
- Feel free to repeat some of the material from the opening phrase: aim to make it interesting but related in some way.
- Decide on the tempo: avoid too many short notes in a fast tempo and too many long notes in a slow tempo.
- End on a relatively long note (a short note may sound unfinished).
- Take care to group the notes correctly when you notate your phrase (see page 9).

The anacrusis

When a phrase begins on a weak beat, it is said to start with an **anacrusis** (sometimes referred to as an '**upbeat**' or '**pick-up**'). The anacrusis can be made up of a single note or a group of notes, and it can start on any weak beat of the bar.

Phrases that start on an anacrusis always finish with an incomplete bar: the first and last bars of the phrase will add up to one complete bar. Thus, a four-bar phrase starting with an anacrusis on beat 4 will still be exactly four bars long, with the phrase ending on beat 3. Similarly, if an anacrusis starts on the third beat of a bar in ¾, the phrase will finish on the second beat of the fourth bar:

Extract from 'Tannhäuser' Overture (1845) by Wagner

Extract from Concerto Grosso in B♭ Op. 6, No. 11 (VI – Gigue) (1714) by Corelli

> The word 'anacrusis' comes from the Greek words *ana* ('up towards') and *krousis* ('to strike'). The term is borrowed from poetry, where it refers to one or more unstressed syllables at the beginning of a line.

Rhythmic transformation

The term **rhythmic transformation** refers to the way in which a short passage of music (rhythmic or melodic) can be transformed by making small changes to its rhythm. Here is an example of a simple one-bar rhythm:

Theory in practice: writing four-bar rhythms

There are several ways to create a four-bar rhythm from a balance of repetition and contrast; here are some starting points you may like to use:

Creating a one- or two-bar rhythm

Write down the rhythm of a word or several words – your name, where you live, what your favourite food is:

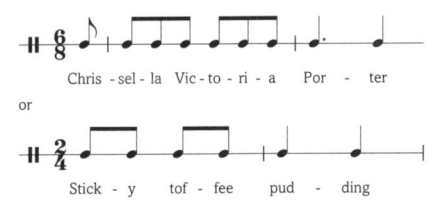

Chris - sel - la Vic - to - ri - a   Por - ter

or

Stick - y   tof - fee   pud - ding

Alternatively, try using a familiar dance rhythm:

Minuet

Tango

Gigue

Developing your rhythm

Once you have selected a rhythm, you will need to extend it to fill four bars in your chosen time signature. There are a number of ways to achieve this:

1 Repeat the rhythm exactly
2 Use the rhythm as a starting point and then alter it slightly
3 Write a completely new, unrelated rhythm.

If you choose option 2, there are certain devices that can be employed (see 'Rhythmic transformation', page 94).

This rhythm can be transformed in several ways:

by splitting longer note values into shorter note values:

by replacing certain notes with rests:

by adding some syncopation:

by doubling all of the note values (augmentation):

by halving all of the note values (diminution):

Developing melodic ideas

Melodic ideas should be developed in the same way as rhythmic ideas – through a combination of repetition, variation and contrast. As well as rhythmic transformations (see above), there are several means of varying a melodic line. Paganini's *Caprice No. 24* (1819) for violin presents some of the devices used to develop melodic ideas, and many composers have created variations on his theme. Here is Paganini's opening melodic fragment:

Here are some ways in which Paganini's music can be varied melodically:

Using sequences: This is a more-or-less exact repetition of a melody at another pitch, either higher or lower. Paganini uses a sequence towards the end of his theme.

Working with rhythm, melody and words 97

Adding decoration or ornamentation: In this example, the first beat has been decorated with a triplet (see page 15). Other ornaments, such as turns and mordents, can also be used to vary a melody (see page 101).

Expanding or contracting intervals: In this example, the interval between the first two notes has been expanded to an octave.

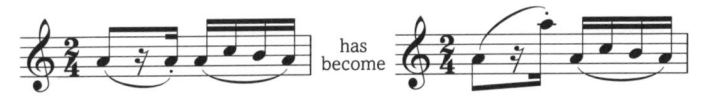

Inversion: This is where a melodic idea is turned upside down. In Variation XVIII of his *Rhapsody on a Theme of Paganini* (1934), Rachmaninov takes part of the melodic idea and inverts it:

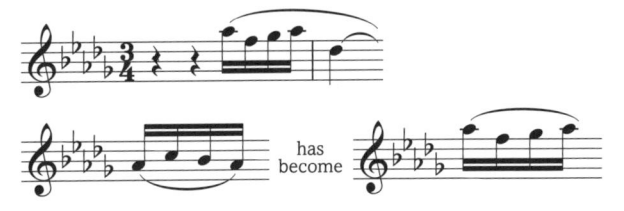

Retrograde: This is where a melodic idea is used backwards. The first bar of Paganini's theme would be written as follows:

> It is also possible to take a melodic idea, use it backwards and turn it upside down. This is known as a 'retrograde inversion'.

> ### Theory in practice: writing melodies
>
> #### Creating your melody
> The overall shape or contour of a melody refers to the way that the notes rise and fall. Good melodies should have a sense of shape and balance and be practical for the instrument performing them.
>
> - Think about the range of notes you would like to use. If you are writing for a particular instrument or voice, take care to pitch the notes within the range of the instrument and to avoid its low and high extremes (see page 76).
> - Consider the structure, length and rhythm of your phrases.
> - Aim to include a balance of ascending and descending movement.
> - Give your melody a sense of direction, perhaps achieving the highest note at an important moment within the phrase.
> - Make your final note either the tonic or one of the notes within the tonic chord. This will make your melody sound complete.
> - Add a tempo marking (and metronome marking) at the start.
> - Add interest using different dynamics and articulation.
> - Add phrase marks.
>
> #### Developing your melody
> Once you have written your melody, there are certain devices you can employ to extend and develop it (see 'Developing melodic ideas', above).

Word setting

The way in which words are set to music is central to creating effective vocal music. The words (or 'lyrics') are taken from existing sources, e.g. poetry, or are written specially for the music.

Rhythm and metre

All text has a natural rhythm and metre, with some words or syllables needing greater emphasis than others. When setting words to music, it is important to use a time signature and rhythm that complements the natural flow of the words. Likewise, the tempo of the music needs to suit both the meaning and the flow of the words.

Syllabic and melismatic word setting

There are two main styles of word setting that can be employed: **syllabic** (one note to each syllable) and **melismatic** (a group of notes to a syllable):

Syllabic

A stream-let clear and sun-ny

Extract from Die Forelle *('The Trout') (1817) by Schubert*

Melismatic

A group of notes sung on one syllable is known as a **melisma**. Melismas are used to emphasise significant words and are commonly found at emotional points in operatic arias.

> When a group of notes is sung on one syllable, a long line is added after the syllable until the end of the last note.

Oh I love_____ you

Word painting

Composers sometimes use a device known as **word painting**, where the music reflects the meaning of the text. In this extract from *Die Forelle* by Schubert, the semiquavers are used to suggest the ripples of the stream:

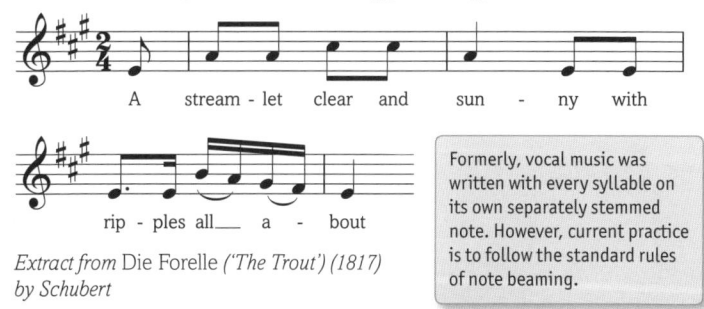

A stream - let clear and sun - ny with rip - ples all__ a - bout

> Formerly, vocal music was written with every syllable on its own separately stemmed note. However, current practice is to follow the standard rules of note beaming.

Extract from Die Forelle *('The Trout') (1817) by Schubert*

Theory in practice: word setting

When setting words to music, it is important to bring out their mood and meaning. Therefore, every aspect of the melody needs to be devised with the words in mind, from the tempo, metre and rhythm to the tonality, melodic shape and dynamics.

Here are some guidelines that may help you with your own word setting:

- Read the words out loud. The sound of the words may suggest duple, triple or quadruple time along with particular rhythms (strong beats and weak beats).

- Keeping the spoken rhythm of the text in mind, mark words or syllables that are naturally accented. This will help you to locate the strong/weak beats and select an appropriate time signature.

  A **stream**let **clear** and **sun**ny
  With **rip**ples **all** a**bout**

  Broadly speaking, stresses should feature on the more important words (such as 'stream', 'sun') rather than on unimportant words like 'and' or 'with'.

- Select one or two of the words that you consider to be most important and decide how to emphasise these (they should already be falling on the strong beats). Consider:
  - shaping the melody so that its climax coincides with this word
  - using a melisma, especially if it is particularly expressive or emotional
  - devising the rhythm, dynamics and articulation so that the word is emphasised.

- When you write down your word setting, make sure that each syllable comes directly under the appropriate note, and use hyphens between syllables of the same word.

Ornaments

'Simple and plain melodies can be lovely. Ornamenting a melody gives it sophistication. In Baroque times it was what you did: a melody was played or sung and the performer would decorate it with appropriate extra notes. Jazz players do the same thing today. Most Baroque and jazz musicians would improvise their ornaments, but learning about them opens up this colourful world of elegance and style.'

Paul Harris

102 Ornaments

Introducing ornaments

Ornaments are notes that decorate a melody. The art of ornamentation was at its height between the sixteenth and nineteenth centuries, when it was regarded as an important element of a performer's technique.

During the sixteenth century, ornamentation was left mainly to the improvisational skill of the performer and was used to vary repeated material, whether whole sections or shorter passages. In the seventeenth and eighteenth centuries, more precise indications were given in the notation. By the nineteenth century, composers often wrote out the ornaments in full. The performance and interpretation of ornaments varies according to the musical period and the speed of the music. No single practice has been followed throughout the centuries, or in any one country.

Ornaments are shown by small notes (sometimes known as **grace notes**) or special symbols. The ornaments in most common use are trills, turns, mordents, appoggiaturas and acciaccaturas.

The trill

The trill (or 'shake') is a rapid alternation of the main note and the note a semitone or tone above it. It often occurs at cadences. A wavy line may be used to indicate the duration of the trill.

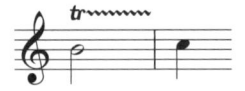

The speed of the alternation of the notes is at the performer's discretion and tends to vary depending on the tempo of the music.

Written *Played*

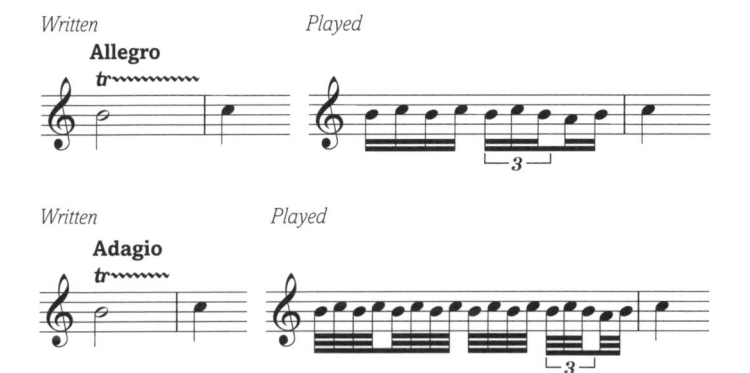

Allegro

Written *Played*

Adagio

Endings

The way that trills are ended is treated differently according to the context of the music. Often it is ended by adding the note *below* the main note before the final main note. This is sometimes indicated by the addition of grace notes, though it is often employed by players even in the absence of written grace notes.

Written

Played

Beginnings

Like trill endings, there are various ways to start a trill, depending on the context of the music. A modern trill (from about 1830 onwards) begins on the main note:

Written

Played

In earlier music (including Bach, Handel and Mozart), the trill begins on the upper note:

Written

Played

When the trill is on a repeated note, it always begins with the upper note:

Written *Played*

Accidentals

An accidental may be placed above the trill to indicate a chromatic inflection:

Written *Played*

The turn

The turn is a type of ornament found chiefly in music of the seventeenth to nineteenth centuries. It is made up of four notes: the note above, the note itself, the note below and the note itself:

Written   *Played*

As a general rule, the turn should be performed fairly rapidly, though the written note values are dependent on the tempo of the music and the placing of the sign:

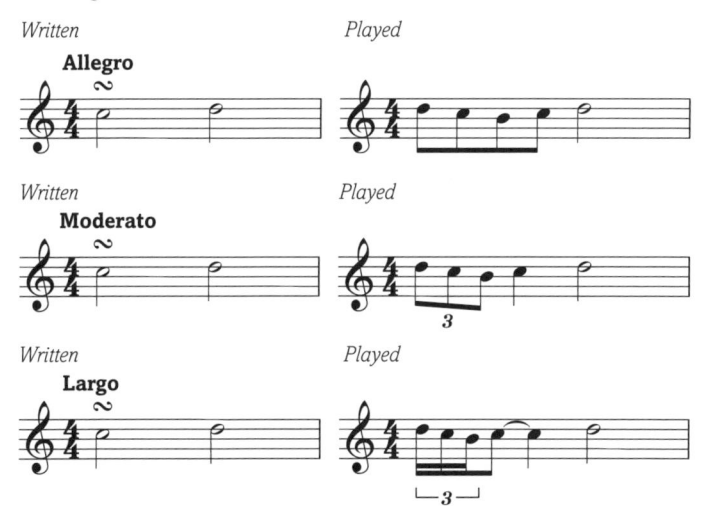

Written   *Played*

Allegro

Written   *Played*

Moderato

Written   *Played*

Largo

The turn is performed *after* the note itself or *instead* of it, according to whether the sign is positioned over the note or after it. When the sign is placed after the note, it may help to think of the ornament as a decoration leading directly into the next note.

Written *Played*

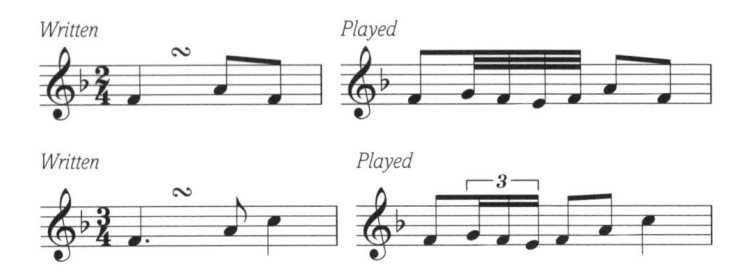

Written *Played*

An **inverted turn** is made up of the note below, the note itself, the note above and the note itself. There are two signs for the inverted turn in common use: ∽ or ∾.

Written *Played* *Written* *Played*

Any accidentals required are placed above or below the sign:

Written *Played* *Written* *Played*

The mordent

There are two types of mordent – the 'upper mordent' and the 'lower mordent'.

The **upper mordent** is made up of the main note, the note above and the main note again, all played as quickly as possible within the duration of the main note:

Written *Played*

The **lower mordent** is made up of the main note, the note below and the main note again, all played as quickly as possible in the time of the main note:

Written *Played*

The interval between the main note and the note above or below is usually a semitone. Sometimes an accidental is placed above an upper mordent sign or below a lower mordent sign to indicate the ornamented note:

Written *Played* *Written* *Played*

The appoggiatura

The appoggiatura is a type of **grace note** sometimes known as a 'leaning note'. It is a dissonant note that 'leans' on a harmony note, taking part of its time value, and is as important melodically as the note on which it leans. It is usually a tone or semitone above or below the main note.

The appoggiatura is shown by a small note (usually a quaver), but the notated duration of this small note need not correspond with the length it has when played. Generally speaking, when played, it takes half the time-value of the main note (or two-thirds of the time-value if the note is dotted).

Written *Played* *Written* *Played*

Written *Played* *Written* *Played*

The acciaccatura

The acciaccatura is a type of grace note sometimes known as a 'crushed note'. It is indicated by a small note with its stem crossed through ♪. Unlike the appoggiatura, the main note here retains its emphasis and almost all of its time-value. The acciaccatura is theoretically timeless and is 'crushed' in as quickly as possible before the main note is heard. It is usually a tone or a semitone above the main note.

Written   *Played*

Arpeggiation

Arpeggiation is where the notes of a chord are spread out: each note is played in turn as quickly as possible, from the bottom note upwards; once a note has been sounded, it is held on until the end of the written chord's duration. Appeggiation is shown by the sign ⦃ and is sometimes known as a 'spread chord'.

The chord may be spread across one stave or two:

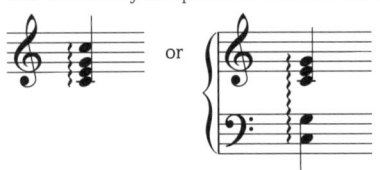

Sometimes the chord is spread from the highest note downwards. This is shown using an arrow-head:

Terms and signs

' 'Follow the signs to the shops', 'No right turn', 'Click to post your message' … The world is full of terms and signs. We need to know what they mean, otherwise things don't happen (or we end up in the wrong place!). Musical terms and signs are useful 'abbreviations' for conveying information. Much can be communicated in a word or a symbol. *V.S. attacca subito* … '

Paul Harris

Tempo indications

Tempo markings indicate the speed at which a piece or section of music should be played. They can be expressed in words (e.g. '**Allegro**') and/or with metronome markings (e.g. ♩ = 120).

A **metronome** is a device that marks time by measuring the number of regularly recurring beats that occur within a minute. This gives players an exact indication of the tempo required.

♩ = 60 indicates a speed of 60 crotchet beats per minute.

♩. = 54 indicates a speed of 54 dotted-crotchet beats per minute.

> The metronome was patented by Johann Nepomuk Maelzel in 1815.

Tempo markings describe the speed and sometimes the character of the music. They are traditionally given in Italian, although they can be in French, German or the composer's own language.

Italian term	Meaning
adagio	slow
adagietto	rather slow
allegro	quick
allegretto	fairly quick, but not as quick as allegro
allegro assai	very quick
allegro ma non troppo	quick, but not too quick
allegro moderato	moderately quick
andante	at a leisurely walking pace
grave	very slow, solemn
largo	broad and slow, stately
larghetto	rather slow
largamente	broad
lento	slow
moderato	at a moderate speed
presto	very fast
prestissimo	extremely fast
vivace, vivo	lively, brisk

A full glossary of Italian terms and signs can be found on page 130.

Tempo changes

Sometimes composers wish to speed up or slow down the tempo of a section of music.

Italian term	Meaning
a tempo	return to the original speed
accelerando	gradually getting quicker
allargando	broadening (getting a little slower)
rallentando (or *rall.*)	gradually getting slower
ritardando (or *ritard.* or *rit.*)	gradually getting slower
ritenuto (or *rit.*)	held back
stringendo	gradually getting faster
tempo primo	return to the original speed
tempo giusto	in exact time

Dynamic markings

The word 'dynamics' is used to describe the varying degrees of loudness and softness at which music can be performed. The standard Italian terms are often abbreviated so that they take up less room on the score.

Abbreviation/sign	Italian term	Meaning
mf	mezzo forte	moderately loud
f	forte	loud
ff	fortissimo	very loud
mp	mezzo piano	moderately quiet
p	piano	quiet
pp	pianissimo	very quiet
cresc.	crescendo	getting louder
decresc.	decrescendo	getting quieter
dim.	diminuendo	getting quieter
$<$	crescendo	getting louder
$>$	diminuendo	getting quieter

These signs are sometimes known as hairpins. $<$ $>$

Qualifying terms

Tempo and dynamic markings can be qualified by the addition of the following Italian terms:

Italian term	Meaning	Example
meno	less	*meno mosso* (less movement, slower)
molto	much, very	*cresc. molto* (gradually get much louder)
più	more	*più mosso* (more movement, quicker)
poco a poco	little by little	*poco a poco cresc.* (get louder little by little)
sempre	always	*sempre forte* (always loud)
subito (or *sub.*)	suddenly	*subito* **pp** (suddenly very quiet)

Other performance markings

As well as markings that indicate the tempo and volume of the music, there are also common terms to describe the character, mood or style of playing:

Italian term	Meaning	Italian term	Meaning
affettuoso	tenderly, with feeling	*grazioso*	gracefully
appassionato	passionately, with feeling	*legato*	smoothly
agitato	agitated	*maestoso*	majestically
amoroso	gently, lovingly	*marcato*	marked, accented
animato	lively, animated	*marziale*	in a military style
cantabile	in a singing style	*pesante*	heavily
con forza	with force	*ritmico*	rhythmically
con fuoco	with fire	*scherzando*	playfully
delicato	delicately	*semplice*	simply, plainly
energico	energetically	*tranquillo*	calmly
espressivo	expressively	*triste*	sadly
giocoso	playfully		

Articulation signs

Slurs (⌒ or ‿) are used to link two or more consecutive notes together. Notes that are slurred should be played *legato* (i.e. smoothly, without any gaps between them) and are positioned above or below the relevant notes. In the following passage, the consecutive quavers (and two crotchets) are slurred together and should therefore be played *legato*:

Extract from Symphony No. 40 in G minor (I) (1788) by Mozart

Phrases are subdivisions of the melodic line (see page 92) and are shown by a type of slur called a **phrase mark**. Notes that appear within a phrase mark should be played in a smooth and connected manner. In the following passage, the eight-bar melody is subdivided into four two-bar phrases:

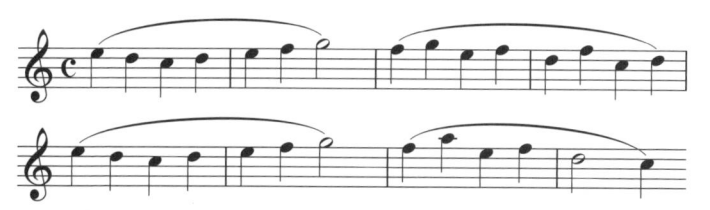

Extract from 'Humming song' from Album for the Young *(1848) by Schumann*

Dots placed above or below the notes should be played ***staccato*** – short, light and detached:

Extract from 'Dance of the Sugar Plum Fairy' from The Nutcracker Suite, Op. 71a *(1892) by Tchaikovsky*

Horizontal dashes placed above or below the notes should be played **tenuto** – slightly stressed and then held on for their full value:

Extract from 'Promenade' from Pictures at an Exhibition *(1874) by Mussorgsky*

Accented notes are marked with an arrow head (>) placed above or below the note head. They should be played with emphasis and a short attack:

Extract from Academic Festival Overture *Op. 80 (1881) by Brahms*

The *fermata*

A **pause** or *fermata* (⌢) placed over or under a note or rest means that the note or rest should be prolonged. The length of the pause is at the discretion of the performer or conductor:

Opening of Symphony No. 5 (I) (1808) by Beethoven

G.P. is short for '**general pause**' and indicates that all performers should be silent, usually for one or two bars. Haydn uses several general pauses at the end of the final movement of his 'Joke' Quartet leading the listener to believe that the piece has finished.

Extract from the 'Joke' Quartet Op. 33, No. 2 (1781) by Haydn

When the abbreviation **8va** or **8** is written *above* notes, they should be performed an octave higher than written. This reduces the number of ledger lines and makes the music easier to read. Here is Tchaikovsky's 'Dance of the Sugar Plum Fairy', notated using the '8va' sign:

> The dashed line indicates the passage that should be played at the higher octave.

Likewise, when **8va** or **8vb** is written *below* notes, they should be performed an octave lower than written.

Repeat signs: section repeats

When a whole section of music is repeated, it is often clearest to use repeat signs (‖: :‖) rather than writing out the same music twice. Repeat signs should be placed at the beginning and the end of the section to be repeated:

> If a repeated section begins at the very start of a piece, the opening repeat sign is not needed.

If a section is played twice, but with a slightly different ending on the repeat, you will need to use **first-** and **second-time endings**.

In this example, the section under ⌐1.⌐ should be played the first time through; on the repetition, the section under ⌐2.⌐ should be played instead. This is how it would be written out in full:

> First- and second-time endings can last longer than one bar and do not have to be the same length as each other. Occasionally pieces use multiple endings.

Da Capo and *Dal Segno* repeats

Da Capo al Fine (or '**D.C. al Fine**') means repeat from the beginning and end at the word 'Fine'.

Da Capo al Coda (or '**D.C. al Coda**') means repeat from the beginning and end by playing the **Coda** (the closing section of a movement or piece).

Dal Segno al Fine (or '**D.S. al Fine**') means repeat from the 𝄋 sign and end at the word 'Fine'.

Dal Segno al Coda (or '**D.S. al Coda**') means repeat from the 𝄋 sign and end at the Coda.

Passage showing a 𝄋 sign

> When *Dal segno* repeats are used, you have to locate the 𝄋 sign earlier on in the piece.

Repetition of bars

The sign 𝄎 means repeat the previous bar:

The sign 𝄎 (with 2) means repeat the previous two bars:

Similar signs can be used for different numbers of bars.

Repetition of ♪s, ♪s and ♪s

A slash through the stem of a note, or above or below a semibreve, tells the performer to play quavers up to the value of that note:

Two slashes through the stem tells the performer to play semiquavers up to the value of that note:

In the same way, three slashes means play demisemiquavers up to the value of that note.

Repetition of pairs of notes

Patterns of alternating notes can be shown by beaming the two notes and placing a short dash inside the beam:

Very fast repetitions of individual or alternating notes create a particular effect known as **tremolo**; composers usually add '*tremolo*' or '*trem.*' when this effect is required.

Appendix 1:
Table of scales and modes

Major scales

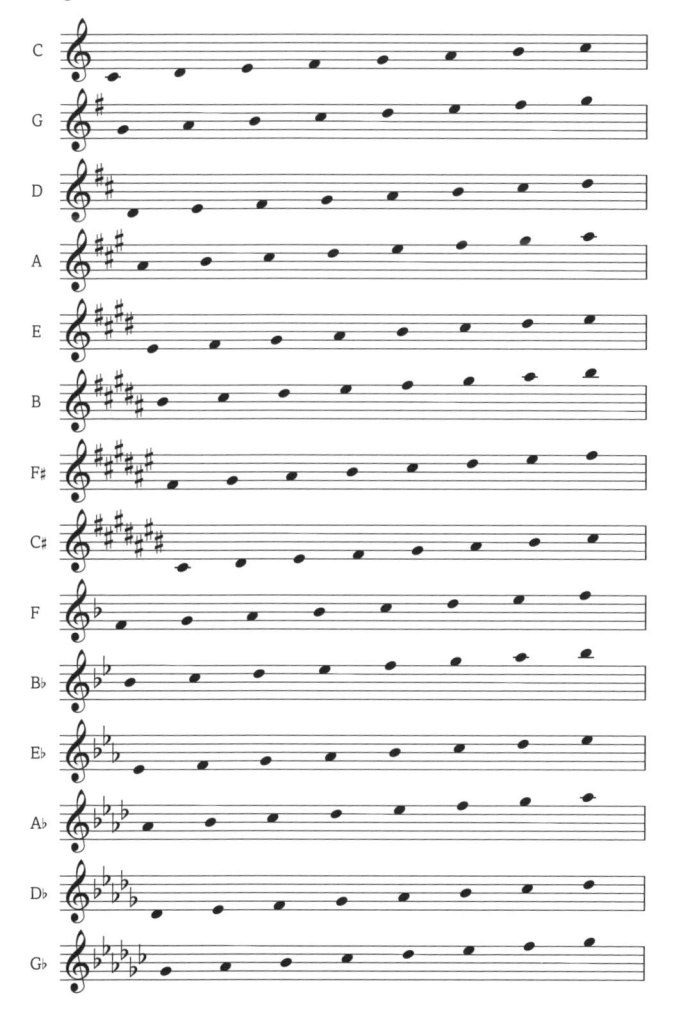

120 Appendix 1

Natural minor scales

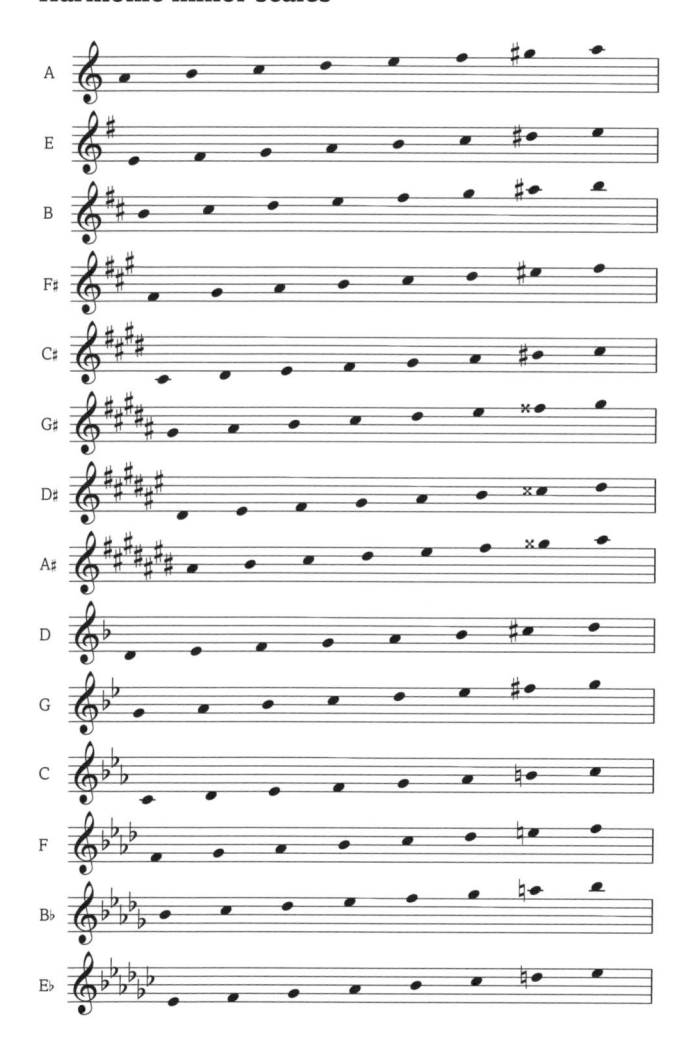

Harmonic minor scales

122 Appendix 1

Melodic minor scales

Main modes

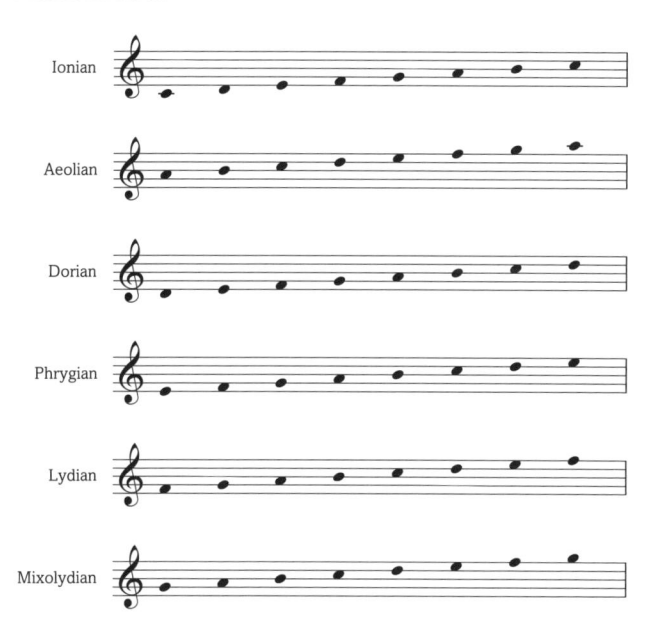

Ionian

Aeolian

Dorian

Phrygian

Lydian

Mixolydian

Appendix 2: Further listening

Pitch

Intervals

The Hungarian composer Béla Bartók (1881–1945) composed *Mikrokosmos* primarily as teaching material. Several of the 153 piano pieces are built on specific intervals. These are:

Book 2 No. 56 Melody in Tenths
   No. 62 Minor Sixths in Parallel Motion

Book 3 No. 71 Thirds

Book 5 No. 132 Major Seconds Broken and Together
   No. 131 Fourths

Book 6 No. 144 Minor Seconds, Major Sevenths

Scales

Melodic minor Beethoven Piano Concerto No. 3 (solo piano, opening bars)

Chromatic Mozart Symphony No. 38 in D ('Prague') (II, opening theme)
   Bartók *Mikrokosmos Book 2* (No. 54 Chromatics, Nos. 91 and 92 Chromatic Invention)

Pentatonic Debussy 'Pagodes' from *Estampes*
   Bartók *Mikrokosmos Book 2* (No. 61 Pentatonic Melody)

Whole-tone scale Stravinsky *Rite of Spring* (Double bass part of 'Dance of the Earth')
   Bartók *Mikrokosmos Book 5* (No. 136 Whole-tone Scales)

Octatonic scale Messiaen *Prélude* (No. 5 *Les sons impalpables du rêve*)

Rhythm

Changing time signatures Copland *Appalachian Spring*
   Bartók *Mikrokosmos Book 6* (No. 142 From the Diary of a Fly)

Quintuple time Holst 'Mars' from *The Planets*
   No. 4 from Shostakovich's *Preludes* for piano (No. 4)

Septuple time Bernstein 'Make a joyful noise' from *Chichester Psalms*
 Prokofiev *Piano Sonata No. 7* (III)
 Bartók *Mikrokosmos Book 4* (No. 113 Bulgarian Rhythm (1))

Triplets Bartók *Mikrokosmos Book 3* (Nos. 55 and 75)

Syncopation Stravinsky 'The Infernal Dance of King Kastchei' from *The Firebird*

Hemiola Bernstein 'America' from *West Side Story*

Working with rhythm, melody and words

Rhythmic transformation Beethoven Symphony No. 5

Melodic transformation Paganini *Caprice No. 24* for violin
 Rachmaninov *Rhapsody on a Theme of Paganini*
 Lutoslawski *Variations on a Theme of Paganini*

Word painting Italian and English madrigals, e.g. Thomas Weelkes *As Vesta Was from Latmos Hill Descending*
 Schubert song cycles, e.g. *Die schone mullerin* and *Wintereisse*

Melisma Handel operas and oratorios, e.g. 'Vivi tiranno' from *Rodelinda*
 Rossini opera arias, e.g. 'Una voce poco fa' from *The Barber of Seville*
 Britten *Serenade for Tenor, Horn and Strings* (on the word 'excellently' in No. 6 ('Hymn'))

Ornaments

The repertoire listed illustrates how ornaments are treated in different musical periods.

Renaissance and baroque *The Fitzwilliam Virginal Book*

Baroque Keyboard works by J. S. Bach, Couperin, Handel and Rameau

Classical Piano sonatas by Haydn and Mozart

Romantic Mazurkas and Nocturnes by Chopin

Instruments and voices

Concertos and solo pieces for each standard orchestral instrument

Flute Quantz, Telemann, Vivaldi, C. P. E. Bach, Danzi, Mozart, Arnold, Nielsen, Rodrigo, Penderecki

Oboe J. S. Bach, Albinoni, Quantz, Telemann, Vivaldi, Handel, Cimarosa, Mozart, Richard Strauss, Vaughan Williams, Britten (*Metamorphoses*)

Clarinet Mozart, Weber, Spohr, Stamitz, Hindemith, Finzi, Copland, Stravinsky (*Ebony Concerto*), Adams (*Gnarly Buttons*), Reich (*New York Counterpoint* for clarinet and tape)

Bassoon Vivaldi, Molter, J. C. Bach, Mozart, Weber, Hummel, Rossini, Jacob, Maxwell Davies, Bingham, Rihm

French horn Telemann, Haydn, Mozart, Schumann (*Konzertstück* for four horns and orchestra), Saint-Saëns, Weber, Richard Strauss, Arnold, Britten (*Serenade* for tenor, horn and strings)

Trumpet Vivaldi, Handel, Telemann, Stamitz, Haydn, Leopold Mozart, Hummel, Neruda, Ponchielli, Pärt, Tamberg

Trombone Wagenseil, Michael Haydn, Leopold Mozart, Rimsky-Korsakov, Jacob, Xenakis, Turnage, Berio, Takemitsu, Bourgeois, Lindberg, Nyman, Pärt, Sandstrom

Tuba Vaughan Williams, Gregson, John Williams, Arnold (*Fantasy* for solo tuba), Hindemith (*Sonata* for tuba and piano)

Violin Vivaldi, J. S. Bach, Mozart, Beethoven, Mendelssohn, Brahms, Schumann, Tchaikovsky, Paganini, Bruch, Elgar, Prokofiev, Shostakovich, Bartók, Berg, Glass, Adams, Gubaidulina

Viola Telemann, Stamitz, Mozart (*Sinfonia Concertante, K. 364*), Berlioz (*Harold in Italy*), Milhaud, Hindemith, Vaughan Williams, Walton, Morton Feldman (*The Viola in My Life*), Schnittke

Cello Vivaldi, C. P. E. Bach, Haydn, Boccherini, Schumann, Dvořák, Saint-Saëns, Villa-Lobos, Elgar, Ligeti, Schnittke

Double bass Dittersdorf, Bottesini, Jacob, Maxwell Davies, Bryars, Henze

Percussion James MacMillan (*Veni, Veni, Emmanuel*), John Cage (*Second Construction*)

Orchestral works using less common orchestral instruments (woodwind)

Piccolo Prokofiev *Lieutenant Kijé*, Debussy *Iberia*

Cor anglais Rossini *William Tell Overture*, Dvořák *New World Symphony*

Contra bassoon Brahms *Variations on a Theme of Haydn*, Ravel *La Valse*

Clarinet in E flat Berlioz 'March to the Scaffold' from *Symphonie Fantastique*

Bass clarinet Richard Strauss *Salome*, Wagner *Götterdämmerung* (Act I, Scene 3)

Solo works using extended instrumental techniques

The twentieth-century Italian composer Luciano Berio (1925–2003) wrote solo pieces using extended instrumental techniques for a range of instruments:

Woodwind *Sequenza I* (flute)
Sequenza VIIa (oboe)
Sequenza IX (clarinet)
Sequenza IXc (bass clarinet)
Sequenza XII (bassoon)

Brass *Sequenza X* (trumpet and piano resonance)
Sequenza V (trombone)

Strings *Sequenza VIII* (violin)
Sequenza VI (viola)
Sequenza XIV (cello)
Sequenza XIVb (double bass)

Piano *Sequenza IVf*

Vocal works

Soprano Purcell 'When I am laid in earth' from *Dido and Aeneas*

Alto Brahms *Alto Rhapsody*

Tenor Puccini 'Nessun dorma' from *Turandot*

Bass Mozart 'O Isis and Osiris' from *The Magic Flute*

Appendix 3:
Periods in music history

Showing the period, with notable composers, forms and styles

Medieval up to c.1450
England Fourteenth/fifteenth century: Dunstable
France Twelfth and thirteenth century: Léonin, Pérotin. Fourteenth century: Machaut. Fifteenth century: Dufay
plainsong, organum, motet, mass, keyboard music, songs and dances

---

Renaissance c.1450–1600
England Tallis, Byrd, Morley, Bull, Dowland, Gibbons
Italy Palestrina, Giovanni Gabrieli, Monteverdi
Netherlands Josquin, Lassus
motet, mass, anthem, Italian and English madrigal, Elizabethan keyboard music

---

Baroque c.1600–1750
England Purcell
France Lully, Couperin, Rameau
Italy Monteverdi, Corelli, Alessandro Scarlatti, Vivaldi, Domenico Scarlatti
Germany Schütz, J. S. Bach, Handel
opera, overture, oratorio, mass, anthem, cantata, fugue, sonata, concerto, concerto grosso

---

Classical c.1750–1810
Austria Haydn, Mozart
Bohemia Johann Stamitz, Carl Stamitz
Germany Gluck, C. P. E. Bach, J. C. Bach, Beethoven
opera, overture, oratorio, mass, sonata, concerto, symphony, concerto, string quartet

Romantic c.1810–1910
Germany Beethoven, Weber, Mendelssohn, Schumann, Wagner, Brahms, Richard Strauss
Austria Schubert, Mahler, Bruckner
Bohemia Dvořák, Smetana
England Elgar
France Berlioz
Hungary Liszt
Italy Verdi
Norway Grieg
Poland Chopin
Russia Tchaikovsky, Rimsky-Korsakov
opera, lieder, overture, sonata, piano pieces, concerto, symphony, string quartet

Early to late twentieth century
Austria Schoenberg, Berg, Webern (Second Viennese School)
England Britten, Cardew, Vaughan Williams
Finland Sibelius
France Debussy, Ravel, Satie, Messiaen, Varèse, Boulez, Xenakis
Germany Stockhausen
Hungary Bartók
Russia Stravinsky, Prokofiev, Shostakovich
USA Ives, Copland, Cage
opera, ballet, music theatre, concerto, symphony, string quartet, piano pieces, impressionism, neo-classicism, expressionism, serialism, electronic, experimental and indeterminate music

Late twentieth century to early twenty-first century
England Maxwell Davies, Birtwistle, Turnage
Estonia Arvo Part
France Boulez
Germany Stockhausen, Kagel, Rihm
Hungary Ligeti
Italy Berio
Poland Penderecki
Russia Schnittke
Scotland MacMillan
USA Cage, Reich, Glass, Adams, Feldman
minimalism, serialism, electronic, experimental and indeterminate music, opera and music theatre, concerto, chamber works, symphony, string quartet, piano pieces

Glossary of common musical terms

Abbreviations: [F] *French* [G] *German* [I] *Italian* [L] *Latin*

a [I] at, to, in the style of
à [F] at, to, in the style of
a cappella [I] unaccompanied choral music
accelerando, accel. [I] gradually getting quicker
adagietto [I] rather slow
adagio [I] slow
à deux [F] for two performers
a due, a 2 [I] for two performers
ad lib., ad libitum [L] freely
affettuoso [I] tenderly, with feeling
affrettando [I] hurrying
agitato [I] agitated
al, alla [I] in the manner of
alla breve [I] with a minim beat
alla marcia [I] in the style of a march, at a marching pace
a comodo [I] at an easy, convenient speed
alla misura [I] in strict time
allargando [I] broadening, getting a little slower
allegretto [I] fairly quick, but not as quick as allegro
allegro [I] quick
allegro assai [I] very quick
allegro ma non troppo [I] quick, but not too quick
allegro moderato [I] moderately quick
amabile [I] tenderly, gently
amore [I] love
amoroso [I] gently, lovingly
amour [F] love
andante [I] at a leisurely walking pace
andantino [I] slightly faster than andante
animato [I] lively, animated
animé [F] lively, animated
a piacere [I] freely, literally at pleasure
appassionato [I] passionately, with feeling
arco [I] play with the bow (a direction following a pizzicato passage)
assai [I] very
assez [F] enough
a tempo [I] return to the original speed
attacca [I] go straight on immediately
avec [F] with
ben, bene [I] well, very
bis [I] twice, indicating the repetition of a short passage

bravura [I] skill, brilliance
brillante [I] brilliant
brillant [F] brilliant
calando [I] getting quieter, dying away
calmato [I] calm, tranquil
calme [F] calm, tranquil
cantabile [I] in a singing style
cantando [I] in a singing style
capriccioso [I] capriciously, in whimsical, fanciful style
cédez [F] yield, slow down a little
col, colla, colle [I] with
colla parte [I] follow the solo part closely
colla voce [I] follow the voice part closely
col legno [I] with the wood, a direction to a string player to play with the wood of the bow rather than the hair
come [I] as, similar to
come prima [I] as before
con [I] with
con bravura [I] in a brilliant style
con brio [I] lively, with energy
con forza [I] with force
con fuoco [I] with fire
con grazia [I] gracefully, elegantly
con moto [I] with movement
con sordini [I] with mute
corda, corde [I] string, strings
crescendo, cresc. [I] getting louder
da [I] from
da capo, D.C, [I] from the beginning
dal segno, D.S. [I] from the sign
deciso [I] decisively, with determination
decrescendo [I] getting quieter
delicato [I] delicately
diminuendo, dim. [I] getting quieter
divisi, div. [I] divided, a direction to players (often strings) to divide into two groups
dolce [I] sweetly
dolente [I] sadly, mournful
doppio movimento [I] twice as fast
douce, doux [I] sweetly
e, ed [I] and
en animant [F] becoming more lively

energico [I] energetically
en pressant [F] hurrying on
en retenant [F] getting slower
en serrant [F] getting quicker
espressivo, espr. [I] expressively
et [F] and
etwas [G] rather
expressif [F] expressively
f [I] see *forte*
facile [I] [F] easily
felice [I] happy
ff [I] see *fortissimo*
fin [F] end
fine [I] end
fliessend [G] flowing
forte [I] loud
fortissimo [I] very loud
forzando [I] with force, emphatically
fp [I] loud, then immediately quiet
fröhlich [G] joyfully
furioso [I] tempestuously, vigorously
gesangvoll [G] in a singing style
geschwind [G] quick
giocoso [I] playfully, humorously
giusto [I] exact
glissando, gliss. [I] a slide
G.P. general pause, indicates that all performers should be silent, usually for one or two bars
gracieux [F] gracefully
grandioso [I] grandly
grave [I] very slow, solemn
grazioso [I] gracefully
joyeux [F] joyfully
lacrimoso [I] sadly (literally 'tearfully')
lamtentoso [I] lamenting
langsam [G] slow
largamente [I] broadly
largo [I] broad and slow, stately
larghetto [I] rather slow
legato [I] smoothly
lebhaft [G] lively
leggiero [I] lightly
légèrement [F] lightly

leicht [G] lightly
lent [F] slow
lento [I] slow
liberamente [I] freely
librement [F] freely
l'istesso [I] the same
l'istesso tempo [I] at the same tempo, sometimes used with a change of time signature to show that the value of the beat remains the same
loco [I] at the normal pitch
lontano [I] distant
lunga [I] long
lunga pausa [I] long pause
lusingando [I] soothingly
lustig [G] cheerful
ma [I] but
maestoso [I] majestically
main [F] hand
main droite [F] right hand
main gauche [F] left hand
mais [F] but
mano [I] hand
mano destra [I] right hand
mano sinistra [I] left hand
marcato, marc. [I] marked, accented
martellato [I] strongly accented
marziale [I] in a military style
mässig [G] at a moderate speed
meno [I] less
meno mosso [I] less movement, slower
mesto [I] sadly
mf [I] see *mezzo forte*
mezzo [I] half
mezzo forte [I] moderately loud
mezzo piano [I] moderately quiet
misterioso [I] mysteriously
misura [I] measure
mit [G] with
moderato [I] at a moderate speed
modéré [F] at a moderate speed
moins [F] less
molto [I] much, very
morendo [I] dying away
mosso [I] with movement, animated

moto [I] movement
mp [I] see *mezzo piano*
muta [I] change, e.g. from B♭ clarinet to A clarinet
nicht [G] not
niente [I] nothing
nobilmente [I] nobly
non [I][F] not
obbligato [I] literally obligatory, used to indicate that an instrument is essential
ossia [I] or, alternatively – often used to indicate a simpler version of a difficult passage
ostinato [I] a constantly repeated rhythmic or melodic pattern
ottava [I] octave
p [I] see *piano*
pausa [I] a pause
pedale [I] pedal
per [I] by, for, through, to
perdendosi [I] dying away
pesante [I] heavily
peu [F] little
piacevole [I] pleasantly, smoothly
piangevole [I] sadly, plaintively
piano [I] quiet
più [I] more
piu mosso [I] more movement, quicker
pizzicato [I] plucked with the fingers
placido [I] calmly, peaceful
plus [F] more
poco [I] little
poco a poco [I] little by little
poco a poco cresc. [I] get louder little by little
pochissimo [I] very little
poi [I] then
pp [I] see *pianissimo*
pianissimo [I] very quiet
ponticello [I] the bridge on a string instrument
portamento [I] a slide from one note to the next
possibile [I] possible
precipitando [I] rushing, headlong
presto [I] very fast
presto possibile [I] as fast as possible
prestissimo [I] extremely fast
prima volta [I] first time

ralentir [F] gradually getting slower
rallentando, rall. [I] gradually getting slower
rasch [G] quick
rascher [G] quicker
retenu [F] held back, a little slower
rinforzando, rfz, rf [I] reinforced, with emphasis
risoluto [I] determined, resolutely
ritardando, ritard. or rit. [I] gradually getting slower
ritenuto, rit. [I] gradually getting slower
ritmico [I] rhythmically
rubato, tempo rubato [I] with some rhythmic freedom (literally 'robbed time')
ruhig [G] calmly, peacefully
sans [F] without
scherzando, scherzozo [I] playfully
schnell [G] quick
sec [F] dry, without resonance
secco [I] dry, without resonance
seconda volta [I] second time
segue [I] go straight on
sehr [G] very
semplice [I] simply, plainly
sempre [I] always
senza [I] without
senza misura [I] in free time
senza sordini [I] without mute
serrer, serrez [F] gradually getting faster
sforzando, sforzato, sfz, sf [I] accented, with emphasis
simile, sim. [I] continue in the same way
slargando [I] getting slower
slentando [I] getting slower
soave [I] smooth, gentle
solenne [I] solemnly
sonoramente, sonoro [I] with a rich tone, resonant
sonore [F] with a rich tone, resonant
sordini, sord. [I] mute
sospirando [I] sighing
sostenuto [I] sustained
sotto [I] below
sotto voce [I] in an undertone, literally below the voice
spicatto [I] a bowing technique in which the bow bounces lightly upon the string
spiritoso [I] with spirit

staccato [I] lightly, short and detached
strepitoso [I] loudly, boisterously
stretto [I] gradually getting faster
stringendo [I] gradually getting faster
subito [I] suddenly
subito pp [I] suddenly very quietly
sul, sulla [I] on the
sul G [I] play on the G string (sul A play on the A string, etc.)
sul ponticelli [I] play near the bridge
tacet [L] silent
tempo [I] speed
tempo primo [I] return to the original speed
tempo giusto [I] in exact time
teneramente [I] tenderly
tenuto [I] held on, sustained
tre [I] three
tranquillo [I] calmly
tre corde [I] release the left pedal
tremolando [I] trembling, quivering, the rapid reiteration of a single note or alternation of two notes
tremolo [I] string players, play with rapid bow movements to produce a quivering effect
très [F] very
triste [I][F] sadly
troppo [I] too much
tutti [I] all, usually a direction to indicate that all performers take part
una corda [I] press the left pedal
und [G] and
una [I] one
unison, unis. [I] in unison, everyone performing the same notes
veloce [I] swift
vif [F] lively
vigoroso [I] with emphasis and spirit
vite [F] quick
vivace [I] lively, brisk
vivement [F] lively, brisk
vivo [I] lively, brisk
voce [I] voice
voix [F] voice
volti subito, V.S. [I] turn the page immediately
ziemlich [G] moderately

Index

accents and accented notes 5, 17, 100, 114
acciaccatura 102, **108**
accidentals 23–5
– and chords 51
– and figured bass 56
– and key signatures 45
– and ornaments 104, 106, 107
– in short score 90
– in transposition 66, 67, 68
Alberti bass 63
alto clef 22–3, 67
Amen cadence 59
anacrusis 94
appoggiatura 102, **107**
arpeggiation 108
arpeggio 63
articulation signs 113–14
augmented chords (see chords)
augmented intervals (see intervals)
auxiliary notes 62

Baroque music 18, 56, 84, 85, 86, 125, **128**
bars and bar lines 4, 5
bass clef **21**, 22, 23
beaming **9–10**, 12, 15, 16, 99, 118
brass band instruments 72, 87
broken chords (see chords)

cadences 57–9
canon 61
chaconne **60**, 62, 63
chamber music and chamber groups 86, 87
chromatic notes 46
chromatic scales **45–6**, 124
chords 49–62
– augmented chords 51
– broken chords 62
– chord layout 60
– dominant seventh 53
– doubling notes in chords 53
– inversions 55
– naming chords 54–55, 56
– pop and jazz chord notation 57
– primary triads 44, 51
– Roman numerals 55
– root of a chord and root position 50, 53
– secondary triads 51
– seventh chords 52, 55
circle of fifths (cycle of fifths) 44
Classical music 63, 86, 125, **128**
clefs 20–22, 23, 67
common time 6
compound time **6–7**, 12–13, 14, 15, 17
contrapuntal texture 61
crescendo 111, 131

da capo 116, 131
decoration 97, 101–08
degrees of the scale 36
diatonic 36, 46
diminished chord (see chords)
diminished interval (see intervals)
diminuendo 111, 131
dotted notes and rests 4, 6–7, 12, 13, 14, 107
double dotted notes and rests 4
double sharps and flats 25
double stopping 82, 83
duple time 5
duplet 15–16
dynamic markings 89, 90, **111–12**

enharmonic equivalent 24, 25, 40, 44
enharmonic intervals 31

fermata (pause) 114
figuration 60, 63, **64**
figured bass 55–6
first inversion 55, 56
flat keys 40, 43

flats 23–5
full close 58

G. P. (general pause) 114, 132
grace notes 102, 103, 107, 108
grouping of notes 9–13
- grouping notes in simple time 9–11
- grouping notes in compound time 12–13

grouping of rests 13–15
- grouping rests in simple time 13
- grouping rests in compound time 14
- whole-bar rests 15

half close 58
harmonic minor (see scales)
harmonic rhythm 60
harmonising notes 60–64
harmony 49–64
hemiola **18**, 125
homophonic texture 60

identifying keys 45
imperfect cadence 57, 58, 59
instrumental ensembles 86–8
instruments 73–88, 125–27
- brass 78–9, 126, 127
- keyboard 84–6, 127
- percussion 80–81, 126
- strings 82–3, 126, 127
- transposing instruments 70–72
- woodwind 74, 76–7, 125–26, 127
interrupted cadence 57, 59
intervals 25–34
- table of intervals 29
- table of musical examples 32–3
- augmented intervals 27, 31
- compound intervals 30
- consonant intervals 31
- diminished intervals 27, 31
- dissonant intervals 31
- harmonic intervals 25

- major intervals 26
- melodic intervals 25
- minor intervals 26
- naming and writing intervals 28, 30
- perfect intervals 26, 27
- recognising intervals 32–4
irregular time divisions 8
Italian terms 110–12, 130–37

key signatures 38–9, **45**
- table of key signatures 43

leading note **36**, 37, 46, 51, 58
ledger lines **22**, 38, 115

major interval 26
major scale (see scales)
measure 4, 5
melisma **99**, 100
melodic inversion 97
melody writing 91–5, **96–8**
metronome markings 110
middle C **21**, 22–3, 67
minor interval 26
minor scale (see scales)
modes 123
- table of modes 41, 123
- Aeolian 123
- Dorian 37, 123
- Ionian 123
- Lydian 123
- Mixolydian 123
- Phrygian 123
modulation 44
mordents 97, 102, **106–07**

natural (accidental) 23–4
natural minor (see scales) 40, **41**, **120**
non-essential note 62

octave **26**, 31, 33, 36
open score 89–90

ornaments 101–08

passing note 62
pause (fermata) 114
perfect cadence 57, 58, 59
perfect interval (see intervals)
performance directions 78, 83, 85
periods in music history 8
phrases 92–4, 98, 113
pitch 19–34
pizzicato 83
plagal cadence 57, 59
polyphonic texture 61, 89
primary triads (see chords)
pulse 1, 5

quadruple time 5
quadruplet 17
quintuple time **8**, 124
quintuplet 15, 16–17

range of instruments and voices
- brass 78–9
- percussion 80–81
- strings 82
- voices 88
- woodwind 76

related keys
- relative major key 43
- relative minor key 43

Renaissance music 84, 85, 92, 125, **128**
repeat signs 115–18
- da capo repeats 116
- dal segno repeats 116
- repetition of bars 117
- repetition of notes 117–18
- section repeats 115

rest signs 2, 4
retrograde 97
rhythm 1–18
- writing four-bar rhythms 92, 94, **95**
rhythmic transformation 94, 96, 125

Roman numerals 55
Romantic period 125, **129**
root of a chord (see chords)
root position (see chords)

scales 35–48, 119–22
- table of major scales 119
- tables of minor scales 120–22
- chromatic 45–6
- harmonic minor 41–2, 121
- major 26, 36, 37, 39–40, 119
- minor 36, 40, 120–22
- melodic minor 42, 122
- natural minor 41, 120
- octatonic 48
- pentatonic major 46–7
- pentatonic minor 46–7
- whole tone 48

second inversion 55, 56
semitone 36–7
septuplets 16–17
sequence
- chord sequence 60
- melodic sequence 96

seventh chords 52–5
- dominant seventh 53, 55
- half diminished seventh 53
- major seventh 53
- minor seventh 53

sextuplets 15, 16–17
sharp keys 39, 43
sharps 23–5
short score 90
simple time 5–6
slurs 15, 16, **113**
sound production of instruments
- brass 78
- keyboard instruments 84, 85, 86
- percussion 80
- strings 82
- voice 88
- woodwind 74

split common time 6
staccato **113**, 136
stave 2, **20**, 22, 89, 90
stems of notes **22**, 90, 99, 108, 117
syncopation **17–18**, 96, 125

tempo markings 110–12
tenor clef 22–3, 67
tenuto 114, 136
texture 60–61
tied notes **4**, 11, 13, 24
time signatures 5–9
− simple 5–6
− compound 6–7
tone 36–7
tonic major 44
tonic minor 44
tonic triad 50
transposing instruments 70–72
transposition 65–72
treble clef **20–21**, 23, 67

tremolo 83, 118, 136
triads 42, 44, 50–52, 53–4, 63
trills 102–04
triple time 5
triplet 15, 17, 125
tritone **27**, 32
turns 97, 102, **105–06**
Twentieth- and twenty-first-century music 127, 129

unison 31, 136

vocal ensembles 88–9
voices 88
− range of voices 88

word painting 99, 125
word setting 98–100
− melismatic 99
− syllabic 99
writing four-bar rhythms 92, 94, **95**